YOUR FINANCIAL FREEDOM IN SIGHT

Property Investment to Bridge the Pension Gap

STEVE EVANS

First published in 2014 by Steve Evans Publishing, England.

Author's photograph by www.theheadshotguy.co.uk.

British Library Cataloguing in Publication Data.

A catalogue record for this book is available from the British Library.

Paperback edition ISBN 978-1-500716-54-7

ACKNOWLEDGEMENTS

This book would never have happened if it weren't for three brilliantly supportive and very helpful people.

Firstly, my wife Catherine who has put up with me being completely absorbed and single minded - to the exclusion of all other jobs and issues that I would have normally taken care of. She has also been brilliant at being there to help with my appalling spelling whilst at the same time keeping her natural talent for the English language and perfect grammar quiet so that you heard my voice rather than that of a good writer.

Then there was our wonderful friend Shila Nadar – Shila is a very skilled linguist and has a huge talent for the English language and the written word. She has spent many an unpaid hour reading through and giving me feedback on whether the text makes sense to someone who has never bought property – an invaluable contribution indeed.

Lastly, my coach, Kevin Bermingham founder of The Successful Author. Without Kevin's amazing system of project managing there is no way you would have this book in your hand today. Kevin got all my thoughts into order and kept me on track the whole way – without his help I would have fallen behind and taken years rather than a couple of months to complete the project.

CONTENTS

Introduction   1

   Why you Should Read This Book   1

   Why I Wrote This Book   7

   How This Book Can Help You   12

   Steve's Top Tips   14

Chapter 1: You Can do it With Your Eyes Shut 17

   Time is Running Out   17

   You Need to Create Long-Term Cash Flow 23

   Anyone can Easily Invest in Property   26

   Exploit Your Assets 31

   You Don't Have to be a Genius, Just Follow
      the System   34

   Summary 36

   Steve's Top Tips   37

Chapter 2: Long-Term Cash Flow Strategy   39

   Why is Strategy Important? 39

   What is Important to Know?   44

   Putting it into Practice   52

   Summary   65

   Steve's Top Tips   66

Chapter 3: Hunting for Bargains   69

   Why Do You Need a Bargain?   69

   What You Should Know   71

   How to Find below Potential Value
      Properties   73

   Summary   84

   Steve's Top Tips   85

Chapter 4: Acquiring Long-Term Assets   87

   Why Buy & Refurbish?   87

   To Gain Control of the Asset   87

   Acquiring a Property   92

   Refurbishing a Property   97

   Summary   101

   Steve's Top Tips   102

Chapter 5: Generating Income   105

   Letting   105

What You Need to Know   109

How to Find & Select Tenants   114

Summary   120

Steve's Top Tips   121

Chapter 6: Extracting Capital   125

Why recycle your capital?   125

Extracting Capital   132

How to Refinance   135

Summary   139

Steve's Top Tips   140

Chapter 7: Managing Your Portfolio   143

Why is Management Important?   143

Property Management   147

Tenant Management   151

Strategy Management   155

Summary   158

Steve's Top Tips   160

Book Summary   165

Next Steps   173

About the Author   175

INTRODUCTION

WHY YOU SHOULD READ THIS BOOK

What This Book is About

The welfare state has never been under so much stress. Barely a day goes by when I don't hear an item in the news media talking about how people are frustrated and worried about their pensions. Those working in the public sector are becoming more and more vocal about schemes like "Final Salaries" not meeting their expectations and how the government and other larger employers are not able to pay in the kinds of contributions necessary to produce the income they had been led to believe they would get.

What is the real problem? Is it just about a corrupt banking system? Is it just about traders and fund managers not performing? Well, in my opinion it isn't any of these things. I believe that the real problem is man's success, man's huge strides forward in the battle against disease and illness. The problem is simply that we are living longer; most people in the developed world can reasonably expect to live until they are in their 80s. That's at least 20 years after retiring. You need an extremely big pot of gold with massive returns on it to keep you in the manner to which you have become accustomed. On top of that it needs to keep up with inflation.

Of course the only way the government can deal with the shortfall is to get people working longer, contributing more and trying to persuade us to pay more in from the start.

And so it is for the small-business owner, we are promised that for every pound we contribute the government matches it. Trouble is, as busy business owners we don't start paying in until we're established and getting cash flow, or, as I did, we start paying in and then something happens and we can't for a while, then we pay a bit more in when we can and then something else happens and we stop again. At the same time, the government changes the goalposts. The retirement age goes up, you can't invest in this or that anymore, and when your pension does finally mature you've got to figure out what to do with it. Should you invest it yourself or trust someone else with it?

I believe that it's time for us to grow up and stop waiting for successive governments and state systems to take care of us. We don't need that now, we need to take responsibility for ourselves, and we need to work out how we can make our own arrangements for our own future and that of our families. For me the solution has been to invest in property, and you are going to learn about why I love property so much. You will discover the three reasons why property in the UK is a sound investment! You will find out how following a simple formula, anyone with half a brain can create an income-generating, capital-building portfolio of their own! And you will learn some simple basics about how you need not pay tax on your investment for the first few years of setting it up!

Why do we have to do it?

What's it all about?

Somebody famous once said "Turnover is vanity, cash flow is sanity". I'm sure that, like me, you've met people who say, "I had a great business once.

I was turning over £3m a year. Then it all went wrong, the tax man and the accountant took it all away from me". I'm sure that in some cases there are good reasons why businesses go wrong; I'm also sure that when people concentrate on turnover and don't pay attention to the cash flow, they will suffer.

The whole point of retirement is to have a comfortable time, living out your remaining years enjoying yourself, doing whatever you want and having enough money to be able to do it, right? In order to do that you need some sort of vehicle, some sort of income producing pot. Oh, and wouldn't it be rather nice if that pot would never, ever, until the end of time, run out?

Well, stick with me throughout this book and you will discover that I have the perfect vehicle to do just that!

At the time of writing I am sitting in my own house, which is paid for, I have a portfolio which is generating over £60,000 turnover and the income from that is rising each year as the costs associated with purchase and refurbishment diminish. And I no longer tune pianos, calculating my hourly income after travelling to and from venues. And

I'm only just in my early 50s having been working full-time in property for three years!

Now I'm going to tell you how I did it. I will show you how to buy property that generates instant cash, I will show you how, with the same property, you can get at least £200 per month, after all expenses – and that's the bare minimum; I will talk about making at least twice that out of one house.

You're going to learn that the systems I talk about can be repeated over and over; just like the yew tree, it's self-perpetuating and can live on after you.

Who This Book is For

This book is aimed at small-business owners, people who feel like they can see no option other than to keep on working and hope they don't fall over. It is designed to help those who think that they have left it too late to start putting money in to a pension to see that they can start to make their own retirement plans.

It is massively helpful for you if you are either not in a relationship, or in a relationship that is supportive – one where the partner will accept and understand what you want to achieve. You are far better off if you can make quick, uncomplicated decisions and remain committed to the goals you set for yourself.

Insufficient Retirement Income

This book is for those of you who look at your pension statements every year and think, "What's going on? I put all this money in and it's not getting any bigger!" Do you ever look at the predictions for what it will pay you and wonder how you will ever live the life you want on the money it'll give you? I know I did.

It's for those who think, "This isn't how they told me things would turn out when I took out my plan!"

Working too Hard for Your Current Income

I'm also talking to you if you feel you are working crazily long hours for not enough pay! How long are you at the "coal face?" Do you feel that if you're not there, nothing will get done? Do you find that if you want something done properly you have to do it yourself?

Can you go away on holiday for three weeks and the business will carry on paying you? Most of the small-business owners I have known can't. They can barely take a week off, and when they do they spend the next week burning the midnight oil, fire-fighting and catching up!

WHY I WROTE THIS BOOK

I wrote this book because I found a better way; I got out before the going got too tough! I took action and am living proof it can be done! AND I WANT TO HELP YOU DO THE SAME!

Notes: What qualifies me to write this book? Let me tell you about myself... From being stuck to being free.

Who am I?

My name is Steve Evans, and I'm going to tell you my story; a story of how I turned my fortunes around by getting educated and following a simple system. I'm going to show you that even if you have a disability such as mine you can still make money and live a great life of financial freedom!

My Qualifications & Experience

Because I had been listening to the likes of Robert Kiyosaki, Napoleon Hill and Tony Robbins, I knew that if I wanted to get anywhere in life, I had to get educated. I tried various "get-rich-quick" schemes, MLM (multi-level marketing) plans, and internet marketing plans, and none of them worked for me. I found that as soon as I got somewhere, things changed and I had to learn all over again.

At the same time, I was seeing one or two presenters on the speaking circuit talking about property investment. They made a lot of sense to me. I had owned property since I was 23, I had seen it go up in value and I wondered if there was any way of keeping what I had and adding to it.

I chose my training mentors and got stuck in. I spent hundreds of hours and probably in excess of £25,000 learning from the best and most successful training company in the UK – seriously, these guys have joint ventures worth over £25 million.

I now have my own portfolio worth about £1,360,000, and it's currently generating over £60,000 a year in rental turnover.

My Story

Life hasn't always been this good. I used to make my living as a piano tuner, exchanging my time for not very much money. When I started out I thought

I would be building a business, but after doing it for over 20 years I just watched the profession die as technology took over.

"How interesting, why did you choose that?" I hear you exclaim.

It's really very simple: when I was born it was discovered that I had a rare eye condition which would render me totally blind. Although I had some useful vision at primary school, I very quickly fell behind the other kids. By the time I was eight years old, my wonderful pushy and determined mum got me registered blind, meaning I would have to go to a school that taught using Braille, white canes and a lot of audio.

As I headed towards the end of my school days, I started to think about my options. I was great at sport, good at music and rubbish behind a desk! I wanted to be a sound engineer, but no one took that seriously. They just said "How would you tell the difference between a blue wire and a black wire?" I wanted to be a physiotherapist but they said "You need three A-levels to do that!" That wasn't going to happen.

In the end piano tuning was introduced to me and

I flourished. I loved the idea of being self-employed and building my own business.

I left school in 1978 and joined the Royal National College of the Blind in Hereford to study piano tuning. In 1981 I qualified with honours and set out in the big wide world. I was invincible; I was going to set the world alight!

Looking back, it is so obvious to me that just working as hard as you can for as many hours as you can will never be a business. I now know that a business is something you create that earns you money even when you are not there, even when you are on holiday, even when you're asleep!

Things went very well to start with. I advertised in the local paper, I tendered contracts, and when I got really successful I took out ads in the Yellow Pages.

Still in my early 20s, I bought my first property and I even took out my first pension plan – how forward thinking is that? I remember the salesman saying "You'll actually be able to take out half the money when you're 50". Well, that's been cancelled by the present government. I think it was when I was about 49 that they raised the minimum age to 55.

During the ensuing years I have watched property double in value on average every 10 years – that first flat I bought for £34,000 is now worth £360,000 30 years later.

During that same time I have seen pensions rise for a bit and then plummet. After starting and stopping my contributions for various reasons over the years, I got an IFA to pull together three separate policies. He found that I had £36,000, so we put that in to one policy and it grew to £41,000, then down it went. It bottomed out at about £21,000 – no way was I going to continue to pump money in to that kind of loss!

Instead, I pursued my dream, my passion, and that was to find something that I could do to generate regular, recurring income that didn't require me to go out every day and do something physical that people would pay me once for and then I'd have to do it all over again to get any more money. No, there had to be something else, something self-perpetuating, something I could do just once, which would pay me over and over again.

Of course, people pay rent every month, they live in the same house for years at a time, so all I had to do was to get them paying their rent to me. All I had to do was to learn how to buy the right properties at the right price in the right location! Sounds simple? Well, it is, once you have learnt the system. Get that right and the rest will follow.

HOW THIS BOOK CAN HELP YOU

"By taking no action, you are taking action not to do something, and that means you are taking the action to let someone else decide your fate!" —Steve Evans.

Okay, so you're a busy business owner and you're doing fine, but you are aware that your retirement plans are not up to speed. How will reading this book help you? Well, I'm going to show you how, by building a modest property portfolio, you can create an extra income and leverage the capital growth to give you additional and recurring income, *forever!*

Too Busy

"But Steve, I'm way too busy to do all that myself!" I hear you saying.

Well, I'm also going to spend some time getting

across the concept of *leverage*. Using other people's time, money and services.

Not Enough Cash

"WHAT ABOUT ME? I DON'T HAVE ENOUGH CASH!"

For those of you who don't happen to have £50,000 sitting around in the bank, we'll look at joining forces, using other people's money.

Here's a Successful Solution

Around about 20 years after I set up as a piano tuner, I started to realise that things were not looking good for the future. I could see that my pension was failing and the likelihood of me being able to retire with any kind of income was dwindling before my very eyes. So I started to look round at my options; I wanted to find something that would keep on paying regardless of what I was doing. It took about 10 years of trying different things – I am very resourceful, but not being able to see does narrow one's choices and make the whole learning process more challenging. It's been an amazing journey and I have learnt a huge amount – about myself as well as investing in property.

Now would be a good time for me to explain a bit about what system I chose and how it works for me.

The basic principle goes like this:

Find a property that is being sold for less than its potential value – it is possible to find people who need to sell cheaply and quickly. Buy it, refurbish it, and then get it valued at its full potential.

During this process, get tenants in and then hold on to the property for the foreseeable future.

Later we will explore the detail of this strategy and look at a couple of variables.

This system has enabled my wife Catherine and me to move out of south east London; I have given up the piano tuning altogether and we now reside in the lovely county of Cheshire. We are living mortgage-free with very low stress levels.

STEVE'S TOP TIPS

1. Always follow a proven system. Seek evidence that the system someone is promoting works. Look at them and what they are doing and find the proof that it is working.

2. Learn your chosen system and stick with it.

3. Find like-minded people and spend time with them to build a support network.

4. Learn about what can go wrong so that you understand the pitfalls.

5. Keep focused on your goals so that when things aren't going your way, you will know why you are doing it and keep going 'til you're out the other side.

6. Take decisive action, because taking no action isn't an option. By taking no action, you are taking action *not* to do something, and that means you are taking the action to let someone else decide your fate!

YOU CAN DO IT WITH YOUR EYES SHUT

TIME IS RUNNING OUT

There are two old sayings I don't hear much these days, but I think they are totally brilliant for us to think about when talking about investing in property.

"An Englishman's home is his castle".

"Put your money into bricks and mortar and it will be as safe as houses".

I think I may have blended two together to make that second one, but you get the gist.

When I was growing up in the '60s and '70s I was fortunate enough to have parents who wanted to own their own property. I didn't know any other way to start out in life besides planning to buy my own property once I had a viable business. Goal setting wasn't even thought of back then, but it's what I was doing. My first flat cost the princely sum of £34,000. The deposit I put down was about £12,000; I think I sold it for around £70,000 less than 10 years later.

Over the next three decades, property has consistently increased in value. Okay, there have been some bad spots, the beginning of the '90s and most recently the crash around 2008 being particularly bad, but it has always picked up again afterwards.

Looking back, it's easy for me to see why I find investing in property a very simple solution to my own pension shortfall. I've always believed that property will gain in value, I've surrounded myself with experts to advise and act for me, and I've listened to people who I can see are successful. In other words, property has served me very well as I've always maintained a positive outlook and taken advantage of the good points it has to offer.

I'm not saying that you should just go out and do

it. There are good ways to invest and there are bad (very very bad) ways, and some people I have met along the way have been severely stung. However, that has not stopped them; they have just learnt their lessons and got back on the ladder and made massive gains because they know the pitfalls. Luckily for me, I have met and listened to them, and I have met and listened to highly successful people who have taught me their systems – systems that are clearly working. It's these systems I follow and will be taking you through in detail later.

Pension Trap

At the same time as buying that first property, this old head on young shoulders took out a pension. I can still hear the salesman saying to me "You'll even be able to take out a lump sum when you are 50, if you want to". Well, that didn't happen, because before I made it into my 50s the government raised the minimum age to 55, and I expect it will rise again before I reach that age.

One of the reasons for the pension shortfall is that the markets (where your money is invested) have not kept up the kind of performance necessary to produce the returns we used to see. At about the same time that property briefly dropped in value, the markets dropped too – only unlike houses, the markets have never recovered at the same levels. I don't know the exact figures, but I do remember that the FTSE was over 7000 before it crashed in 1987, and it's still nowhere near that level 27 years later.

Did you know that fund managers have to put your money into the markets, regardless of what it's doing? That means that even if the market is nose-diving your money is still in there. The reason for that is quite simple: imagine you're a fund manager and you control £30,000,000 and you pull it all out of the market – just think about the effect that will have on the market…

Unable to Retire from Business

The consequence of the pension turmoil for self-employed small-business owners is that for many it's difficult to ever see themselves retiring. You were expecting to get enough money put away to live off for the rest of your days. The truth is somewhat less attractive. You are trapped between the devil and the deep blue sea. Your pension isn't going to keep you; if you sell your business you lose your income; plus, even if you get a lump sum out, interest rates are so low (lower in fact than the real rate of inflation) that your money is actually losing money whilst it is in the bank!

Hopefully by now you're itching for me to start telling you how to invest in property. Well, I can't wait; it's such an exciting time right now. Suddenly everybody is excited about property again, and this time I'm on the crest of the wave and I'd love you to join me. What do I mean by the crest of the wave? Well, not only is most of my portfolio cash-flowing, i.e., after all the costs (mortgage, insurance, general maintenance and management) they pay me some income. It's now going up in value. Just think, every time you hear newsreaders stating that property has gone up by 3% this month or 14% over the past 12 months, my wife and I are gaining that over the spread of seven properties. If one house goes up by £5,000 that equals £35,000!

If you are a small-business owner aged 45-65, you are in a good position to start investing in property and not worry about pensions and what the government will do to them. Because you have income from your business, it is very easy for you to get the finance. Easier, in fact, than it is for me!

It Takes Time to Build up an Income Stream

There is no time like the present. Like any investment there's a lag between investing and getting your return. Later, we will explore the issues and pros and cons related to good debt and bad debt. For the moment, it's enough to point out that when you first invest and carry out refurbishments you will be running a loss. At this time, you need to utilise your positive mindset and keep your eye on the goals you set yourself. So long as you are following a proven system and you stick to it, you will get your returns. It will take a couple of years before your portfolio starts to pay you back. At this point it is worth mentioning accountants. You may have an accountant who looks after your business accounts perfectly. However, an accountant who specialises in property is a must if you want to take advantage of all the tax breaks you are entitled to as a property investor. I will go on to talk in some general terms about these later.

Goalposts are Moving

There are many advantages of property investing as a strategy to provide yourself with an income in retirement. One of the major benefits is, whatever happens with pensions and whatever successive governments think is the age you should be working to, you can just decide for yourself when you are going to stop working and live off the fruits of your investing! You may decide, like many of my friends and colleagues have, to sack your boss early.

Just imagine reading the headline, "GOVERNMENT RAISES RETIREMENT AGE TO 75". If you've got a portfolio paying you income every month, are you worried? If you're just relying on your pension and you've got to keep working for an extra 5-10 years, how are you going to feel?

YOU NEED TO CREATE LONG-TERM CASH FLOW

Regularity

A massive change in my life, once my portfolio started to cash-flow, was getting regular and recurring income. Before I had investment properties I used to just attempt to live off whatever money I got in at that time, so I was always trying to do more, trying to build up more cash than I needed. Now it's very different. Now I know what I will have coming in every month. All I have to focus on is whether everybody has paid their rent each month.

Security

Okay, so sometimes tenants leave, sometimes there are unexpected maintenance costs; but on the whole, the amount of money coming in every month is consistent. With consistent outgoings and regular income it is now possible to plan ahead.

How Much Cash is Enough?

Only you can decide what is enough. In order to decide that, you need to think about a number of things: Do you want property to be a small subsidy to your pension? What will your outgoings be when you retire? Do you want to live a jet-setting lifestyle or are you happy to stay where you are? What sort of healthcare will you want?

You must think about these issues now in order to know what you are aiming for. This will help you to decide on the size and type of portfolio you need. Once you have made that decision you will know how much work to put into building your investment plan.

Cash v Assets

Now that I've got you thinking about the future, let's start looking at the present. You will already have some assets and cash available to use to build your investments. For the purposes of our kind of investing you need to have a clear understanding of what assets and liabilities are. The definition I like to use comes from one of the most inspiring authors of the personal development world, a man who has changed the lives of thousands of entrepreneurs: Robert Kiyosaki. In his series of books called Rich Dad Poor Dad, he describes a liability as something that costs you money and an asset as something that makes you money. In other words, the house you live in is not an asset; it is a liability because it costs you money and doesn't make you anything. An investment property, one with paying tenants in, is an asset. If you have a car that you use to drive to work, that is a liability. However, if you have a car and you are using it as a taxi, that is now an asset. For a layman this definition is very useful; it keeps us real about where we stand. Accountants would have more to say on the subject of liabilities and assets, but it doesn't help us to know the finer detail. All we need to understand is what assets we can use.

ANYONE CAN EASILY INVEST IN PROPERTY

Investment

Property investing is not complicated. You only need a rudimentary understanding of some very simple basics of market forces. If you understand this next bit on why to invest in the UK then you can do it.

When choosing any type of investment you must consider its potential to make you money. How will it make you money? How much will it make you? What type within that class of investment works best for you?

When investing in property you should ask yourself these questions: What is the demand? Who wants to live in it? How long will they live there? What is the competition?

There are a great many ways to invest in property, and you can spend years looking at all the options. I could write several chapters on what not to invest in, but I find that if I spend time telling people about the downsides to most of them they just ignore me and go off and do it anyway. All I want to say about things like off-plan, new-builds, buying abroad and holiday lets is that there's usually a salesperson involved whose sole intention is to get their commission. They have no interest in whether you are going to make money in the future, only whether they are going to make their bonus next month. I have no problem with salespeople, many of them do a great job and every business needs to have people who can sell it. But for you, the future property investor, you need to have the knowledge and skills to make your own judgement. After all, you're betting your future standard of living and final years of comfort here. If you get it wrong, you won't have the time or the money to reinvest should some developer, abroad or in the UK, run off with your deposit.

I do think it is worth explaining why the UK is such a fabulous place to make money from property. Firstly, demand. The population is growing all the time – most people looking for work and a better way of life want to get into our system. Secondly, supply. Since the Second World War, governments have struggled to build enough houses to keep up with demand, and since The Right To Buy, introduced by Mrs Thatcher's Conservative government in the '80s, stripped the social housing stock of hundreds of thousands of homes, there just aren't enough houses for all the people. Thirdly, the government now needs private landlords, so many are specialising in social housing. Fourthly, there are huge constraints on building: one, we are an island; two, we need land to grow food on; and three, we care passionately about wildlife and our green spaces. My fifth and final point is something new, something that has been bubbling under the surface during the recession and is now exploding all over London and the southeast; it is verification that what I have just stated is true, proof, if ever it were needed, that Britain is perfect for property investment. Foreign investors are pumping billions of pounds into our property, they all want a piece of UK real-estate and they are driving prices up at an alarming rate!

Property

Okay, I think I should have convinced you by now that the UK is the place to be. What about the types of property? There are many to choose from:

Commercial

There are subsections of this, but it's not for the faint-hearted. I am just learning about taking on bigger types of projects, and it's not something I would recommend to the novice.

Domestic

This is where we can really go to town! Within the domestic category there are many subcategories, and this is where you need to start planning your strategy.

Detached

Expensive, but can work mostly as HMO in the right place.

Semi-Detached

Less expensive than detached and could work for either professional single let or HMO, if big enough and in the right place.

Terraced

Very affordable and will work as single let, HMO (if big enough), or they can even be split into flats when very large.

I should just take a moment to describe the types of tenants mentioned in the above paragraph. Single let: one or more related people living as a family unit; Professional let: the same as single but with higher income; HMO (house of multiple occupancy), that is, a house where most of the rooms are bedrooms and each room is rented to an individual tenant.

Types of Investors

The most important consideration when investing in anything at all is, can you afford it? When
investing for yourself you do need to have a pot
of money to get started. It is possible to invest in
property without an initial lump sum, and we will
go briefly into some of those strategies shortly. For
now though, I am just talking about an individual
with £50,000 who wants to do it for themselves. If
that is you and you have it in cash or feel you may
be able to raise it in some way, think about whether having your money tied up somewhere would
cause you cash flow problems. This is vital to think
about, and when I sit down with clients and assess
their affordability we go into a lot of detail about
their income and cash flow. Remember, when you
start to invest, you will have your cash tied up for a
considerable period before the cash starts to flow.

Investing in property doesn't suit everybody. If you
don't own your own property or you don't have
£50,000 available it could be challenging to get
started, and if you want to get involved you should
seek education from some of the training companies you can find online. If you feel that property investors are sharks and getting property at discount
prices is taking advantage of vulnerable people

and isn't fair, then you shouldn't invest in property. If you have CCJs against you it may be difficult to get started. And, if necessary, you should take actions to clear up your credit rating – it is possible and it is well worth tackling rather than ignoring.

Take the Easy Route

The basic principles behind investing in property are very straightforward. I do not have much of a formal education, I have a disability which makes getting around challenging, and most people I talk to think that estate agents would seize the opportunity of my not being able to see to pull the wool over my eyes. Well, none of that has stopped me making a success of it, so there's hope for anybody at all to do this well.

You see, all I have done is find out from successful people how they have done it and copied them.

EXPLOIT YOUR ASSETS

Personal Assets

I've already mentioned Robert Kiyosaki's definition of assets and liabilities being that liabilities cost you money and assets earn you money. You can, however, turn a liability into an asset. If the liability has an intrinsic value, you may be able to utilise that value in order to gain some assets.

For example, look at the things you have around you, your car or your house, what are they costing you? And could you turn them into cash? Is there equity in your home?

Others' Assets

If you don't have anything yourself, you might be able to involve someone else; a family member or a very close and trusted friend. If you need to do that, it is vital that you approach them carefully and in a business-like manner. It might be helpful to give them a copy of this book first and then draw up a business plan to show them what sort of returns they can expect and over what timescale.

Businesses as Assets

I'm not a financial advisor or accountant so I can only speak in general terms, and you should seek the advice of a professional before taking any action. That said, it may be worth looking at your business and asking yourself, "How can I extract some funds out of it?" Here are a couple of thoughts: does the business owe you any money? Now might be a good time to start getting it paid back. Could it pay you more, in order to increase your borrowing power? Do you have any personal possessions it could buy from you? There may be other ways your business could help that I don't know about, so talk to the professionals.

How Best to Exploit Different Types of Asset

*Cash is king...*The whole point of looking at your assets is to see what you can turn into cash – when you have cash you have buying power! I'll leave the most obvious one, your home, to the end, but have you thought about what else you could use? Now that you know that things that cost you money are liabilities, are there some much treasured items that you could do without for now so that you can have bigger, brighter, better ones in the future? What about that status symbol car? Could you downsize and put a couple of grand away to fund your investments? How about that holiday home you only use a couple of weeks a year? If you converted that money into a tenanted property, that could be the beginning of your passive income.

A couple of things to consider there, and I'll leave you to think about them.

Now, what about your home? When was the last time you had it valued? If you live in a major city you may be pleasantly surprised, especially if you live in London. Don't just go on what you hear in the press, you can look at websites such as Rightmove and Zoopla to get an idea, or get a couple of estate agents round to give you up-to-the-minute prices.

There are two ways you can utilise your home: the first is to sell it and downsize, and the second is to borrow against it. If you want to borrow against it you should consider some rather complex tax implications, which are too involved to go into here and differ depending on your required outcome. This is another example of what I go through with clients before setting up their individual strategy.

YOU DON'T HAVE TO BE A GENIUS, JUST FOLLOW THE SYSTEM

Remember I said that when I was at school I didn't do very well once I was behind a desk? I think that's why I do well at property investing. I'm not clever enough to reinvent the wheel, all I have done is get myself educated, learnt some systems and gone out and done it.

Systems Create Consistency & Predictability

One of the world's most successful businesses is very well known for its systems. McDonald's is famous for being a business built on systems. When you take on one of their franchises you get an enormous manual; everything they want the staff to do is written down in the manual and this means that they can employ unskilled staff who produce consistent, uniform food whether they're in New York, London or Mumbai.

All the successful property investors I know follow one system or another, some of which are complicated and others of which are very simple. I prefer simple, so that's what you're going to hear about from me.

Step 1: Strategy

The strategy this book is based on is very simple and I love it because it will work in any market, whether the market is up or down! I call it "PROP": P Purchase; R Refurbish; O Occupy; P Pull your money out. We will go through each of these later.

Step 2: Acquisition

Acquiring the property at the right price is the most essential part of the process. When working with single let investments it is necessary to purchase at a discount, and later you will learn how that is possible even in an upbeat market.

Step 3: Portfolio Management

You will need to decide whether you want to manage your portfolio yourself or use agents. I will talk later about the pros and cons of both.

SUMMARY

This chapter was all about the building blocks. I talked about property being a much better investment than a pension fund. I also looked at assessing your assets and what exactly assets and liabilities are. You learnt that liabilities are any possessions you have that cost you money while assets are possessions you have that earn you money. I also explained that you are an ideal investor if you are a small-business owner with £50,000 cash available and an income of £30,000 or more. And you learnt that you can use equity in your home or raise the money out of your business.

STEVE'S TOP TIPS

1. Positive mindset. By keeping a positive outlook on property you can achieve your goals. Surround yourself with others who are positive and they will help you to achieve your goals.

2. Salesmen's objectives. When talking to salespeople remember that they have targets and goals of their own and they may not be aligned with yours.

3. Spreading the risk. When you've got three or more properties in your portfolio your gains are multiplied: 5% increase on £100,000 is £5,000; 5% on three houses at £100,000 is £15,000.

4. Financial advice. Get an accountant who invests in property themselves; they will have a far better understanding of the issues.

5. Goal setting. Imagine your life when you are 80 – will you be living the life of your dreams? By thinking about yourself in the future you will find the motivation to achieve your goals.

6. What is an asset? Assets are things that earn you money. Your home is a liability because it costs you money...a house with paying tenants in is an asset because it's paying you cash.

7. Raising the money. Downsizing on things like status symbol cars and or your home can generate useful cash.

8. How much is your house worth? You can get an idea from Zoopla or Rightmove, and they actually have sold prices.

LONG-TERM CASH FLOW STRATEGY

WHY IS STRATEGY IMPORTANT?

Big Picture Context

How does a piano tuner who is blind, who lives in Beckenham, Kent, find his way to a house in Knightsbridge, central London? How does that same person find his way to Deal on the Kent coast? Or no. 63 St Botolph's Road in Sevenoaks?

The answer is very simple…I developed strategies for building my mental maps and planning my journeys. Never, in nearly 30 years of travelling around London and the south east, did I fail to turn up at an appointment. I hardly ever asked a client to help me find their house; in fact, most of my clients didn't even know I was blind until I turned up on their doorstep, and most of the time I didn't have a mobile phone, or sat nav!

I'm not trying to show off in any way – just pointing out that because I am blind I have to rely on creating strategies to achieve my goals, and I know lots of very successful, multi-millionaire property investors who've achieved massive goals, much bigger goals than I have ever dreamed of. They all have one thing in common…they all have specific strategies; they are even more focused than me, and I now spend time learning their strategies so that I can achieve even more!

Strategies are crucial for achieving goals that require many steps. The Chinese have a wonderful saying: "A journey of a thousand miles begins with a single step". I say, "You will never reach your destination if you don't have a map".

Failing to Plan, Means Planning to Fail

When I was that piano tuner nobody told me how to do it. How should somebody who can't see road names or door numbers, or even read a map, head off on multiple buses and trains, and walk unknown streets to strangers' houses? I just developed the strategy over time and experience. Believe me, there were many errors along the way, many wrong turns, and quite a few missed bus stops. I could have saved a lot of time if I had paid someone to write down the strategy, and I could then just have followed it and not made all the mistakes along the way.

"Doesn't everybody make plans, Steve?" Well, no. I have met people who talk about all sorts of different things they are doing; one minute its Multi-Level Marketing (MLM), the next it's internet marketing, then it's something else – I've been guilty of it myself too, until I immersed myself in property investing. I'm always seeing evidence of people's inability to plan when I travel on the London underground, for example.

When I make a journey that involves the Tube I have to work out how to get to my required destination. Where am I starting from? What changes do I need to make? Where do I go when I leave the network? The staff have a fantastic strategy for helping people with disabilities. When I arrive at the gate they ask me where I am going, then they go down with me to the platform. While we are walking down they tell the station controller where I am headed, and then when I'm on the train they radio back to the controller the number of the train I am on. When I get to my stop a member of staff is there to meet me and we continue on to the next part of the journey. This is a great example of Transport for London creating a strategy for helping people with disabilities to navigate the network.

Almost every time I go through the Tube network I am amazed at the number of people who attempt to stop the member of staff who is assisting me, to ask the way somewhere, usually a place miles away from where we are. These people set out to go somewhere and have absolutely no idea of how they're going to get there; they have maps and apps, all designed to make it easy, and yet they are clueless on how they will achieve their goals...I often wonder if that's how these people run their entire lives.

Avoiding Shiny Objects

During the dark years – the years when I knew that I had to do something different, something to turn my fortune around whilst I still had energy and time – I tried all sorts of things. I started with network marketing; after all, I spent every day going in and out of people's houses, sitting down with them and chatting over copious cups of tea.

Some bought things from me, a lot didn't. After that I started to get into online affiliate marketing, which was harder, much harder, than the people selling it told me it would be. I also worked for an international business breakfast organisation for six years. And then there was share trading, which really is a challenge when you can't see the chart patterns! None of these things ever showed me the kind of staying power of property. Property was the only thing I could see that would keep me into my retirement, so I started to concentrate entirely on it.

It isn't enough though just to say, "Now I am concentrating on property". You see, whatever you are doing at the moment, you'll meet someone or get an email from someone who is doing something else that they think is great – something new and shiny. Even within property, there are dozens of different strategies, and lots of different ways of doing great deals; some are easy and others are less easy, but most of them will work because they are based on the same fundamental: property. The thing is, unless you are intending to do this full-time, you won't have time for it; you must focus on your chosen strategy.

WHAT IS IMPORTANT TO KNOW?

Setting Goals

Obviously my goal when making a challenging journey is the end destination, so when planning your goal, you must be honest with yourself – are you more like the people I meet on my Tube journeys? Clueless and not knowing how you're going to get there? Or, are you like that blind piano tuner, focused with laser-sharp vision on your destination? Armed with a plan and a strategy for getting there?

We hear a lot about goals these days, and I worry that people don't really take in the importance of setting them. Think about where you want to be in 20 or 30 years' time. Think about who will be with you then. Think about what you want to have then. Think about what you want to give, whether to your family or perhaps to your favourite charity.

Don't Put All Your Eggs in One Basket

When investing, it is important that you have a strategy in which what you might lose on the swings you can gain on the roundabouts. This isn't an exact science and things won't always work out the way you want, so when I work with a client I will always encourage them to spread their risk. By spreading your risk you are not so badly exposed to alterations in the market. By spreading your risk you can buy time for when things change or don't go to plan.

My own portfolio includes a licensed HMO (house of multiple occupancy), two smaller, unlicensed HMOs, and the others are all single lets. They are all purchased using the strategy I am going to explain to you throughout this book, but they are all slightly different to one another in that most are terraced properties, two or three beds, while a couple are semi-detached. One has young professionals as tenants, and the others have blue collar workers in them.

More is Better

There are two excellent reasons for having a portfolio…the first is that when you have a void for any reason, (and there will be a few), the others – the houses that are cash-flowing – will provide you with the funds to keep it going, i.e., they can subsidise it. The other big reason for having your portfolio is something I have already touched on – when property values go up you are multiplying the gains. Quite simply, when you've got three houses worth £100,000 and the market gains 10%, instead of gaining £10,000 you have amassed £30,000! Now that's a very simple bit of maths, and of course you don't get gains like that overnight – I just did it with those numbers to make the picture quite clear, especially for people who, like me, can't keep up with complicated graphs, pie charts or spreadsheets! The point is that the more houses you possess, the more you benefit.

Whenever I talk to clients, friends or relatives, and I mention property values going up, the more astute of them argue that prices will come down as well as go up. While that is very true, it shouldn't matter when a rented house that is cash-flowing goes down in value. If that house is bringing in £200 per month after all expenses you can just keep it; you don't need to sell it, so why worry?

Self-Management or Hands-Free?

The last part of setting up your personal strategy is to decide on how your property is to be managed once it is up and running. There are quite a few issues to consider here. I meet a lot of landlords who moan like billy-o about tenants and, then again, I meet a lot of landlords who constantly complain about letting agents. There's no simple solution to managing property – all I can do is point out the things you need to consider, and then you'll have to make up your own mind.

Where is your portfolio? You may need to travel there each time there is something to deal with. How much time do you have to deal with advertising, viewings, vetting tenants, and writing contracts?

If you want to use an agent you should still learn about the job of managing so that you know whether the agent is doing their job correctly. There are some agents who are lazy and unprofessional, so you must know what they are doing or not doing on your behalf. They may be your representative, but the buck stops firmly at your feet.

Buy, Refurbish, Refinance (My 'PROP' System)

The basic principle behind successful property investing took me a long time to understand. When I got it, it was a real lightbulb moment for me – I suddenly saw money being printed in front of my very eyes! So, if it doesn't make sense to you right now, don't worry as it will when you're ready for it.

At some point further into the book you will get it, and it will all make sense.

This is what good property investing is all about. That is, good *long-term* property investing. I am not talking about flipping (i.e. buying and then selling on at a quick profit). There is nothing wrong with that in the short-term, but you are getting into the realms of capital gains tax as well as potential unsustainability. I am only interested in buying and holding; putting tenants in who are going to stay for several years, thus providing recurring income.

I have called the model this book is built upon 'PROP'.

It's an acronym that should help you to understand the main steps to acquiring your cash-flowing pension pot.

P. Purchase

When you purchase the property, you must buy at a price that generates instant equity. That is, a discount on the potential value of that property. I will explain how to work out what price will work, and how to get discounts, in more depth later.

R. Refurbish
Now that you have your house you need to tart it up, and for two different people. The first is your tenant, and I'm sure you're ahead of me with that one. The second is someone you haven't met yet; this person is very valuable to you and you must impress them otherwise the whole thing falls apart – you will see why in a moment.

O. Occupy
Once you have refurbished and made the house habitable, you need to get your tenant in. You must decide from the very start who your tenant is, because that will determine what sort of house to buy in the first place, and where to buy it.

P. Pull money out
This is the clever part, the part that took me a long time to understand. This is where you can get the property revalued based on what you have done to make it better, and on comparative values of similar properties nearby. This is where you need to impress that other, hitherto unknown party, your valuer.

Demographics

Another key element to your strategy is your tenants – who are they? This will help you to determine what type of property to buy. Now you need to think about many factors that are all interdependent. I found it really helpful when I learnt about yield; having a simple formula to guide you will make choosing your investment area much easier. Later I will show you the method that works for me, and makes working out the price I'll pay for a particular type of property very simple. In deciding where to invest you need to know who is paying what to live where. Then you take your simple yield calculation and see just how close you can get to the magic numbers.

To find out anything about prices, just go online to Rightmove or Zoopla where you can search for property for sale and property for rent – just go and get a feel for what is happening in your area. Think about the correlation between the prices of three-bedroomed houses for sale and rental prices for equivalent properties.

Another important factor to consider is the big employers in your area. If you just type into a search engine something like "biggest employers in *Town*

Name", you will find out all sorts of information (just weed out the job ads and recruitment companies!)

What is Value?

There is no authority or government organisation, no scientific formula or governing body that sets the price of property; it is a free market. Value is determined by the market. People put property on the market and other people come along and try to buy it. The agents try to get the best price for their clients, and so they should. The buyers try to buy at the best price for themselves. That is my description of the free market. Price is determined by market forces – it's simple really. Later, I will explain how we get discounts.

What Specialists are Needed?

When you are trying to get property at a discount it is essential that you can act fast and that you are able to deliver. In order to do this, you must have a couple of professionals in place ready to rock and roll as soon as you have agreed on your price.

The people you must have ready are: a great solicitor, one who understands your need to act fast, and an excellent mortgage broker. Don't try to cut any corners here; these people really know their market and the best ways of taking advantage of offers and exclusive products.

Once you have your property you'll need tradespeople. You might be able to do some of the refurbishment (refurb) work yourself, but I bet there's something you can't do, whoever you are and no matter how clever you are! So get them ready in advance, and know who you need to call and when. The faster your refurb goes, the sooner you can start to get your money back.

PUTTING IT INTO PRACTICE

Setting Goals

I guess by now you may be feeling a little overwhelmed, so let's get back to why you're reading this; why you want to build a property portfolio. You see, without a big enough "why", you will not make it through the tough times. So, you must have a clear picture, you should tune into your goals, and you have to get a strong feeling for them in order to believe you can achieve them.

People have different ways of making their goals stronger and more meaningful for themselves. NLP

(Neuro-Linguistic Programming) teaches us that people think by representing the world around them internally, in their minds, with the five senses. Most of us favour one sense over the others; don't worry too much about the technicalities, just find out what works best for you. Think about a particular goal (best if it's an object), and find out what makes you more excited about it by doing the following: Look at a picture of your goal, listen to someone talking about your goal, or touch it. Which one gets you most excited about it? When you know what gets you turned on with goal setting, do it – do lots of it.

I love this stuff and I could go on for many pages about it. I think having goals is essential to drive us forward, and I believe this is what has got me over the obstacles my disability has put in front of me. The most important thing about setting goals is that you make them big, very big! The bigger you make your goals, the harder you will work to get them! I know, when you've been on workshops or team-building exercises they've told you to make "SMART" goals – specific, measurable, achievable, results-focused and time-bound. Well that's OK for beginners; it teaches you the most basic principles around goal setting which are:

- Decide on your goal – what is it that you want?

- Plan out the steps you'll need to get you there.

- Celebrate getting there.

When you set a goal it should be something challenging. For me right now, it's getting this book written. You should feel a bit daunted at the thought of that goal, so now's the time to think about how you can achieve it. What do you need to do to get there? This is known as "chunking down"; when you have a big target and the only way to get there is to break it down into smaller, bite-size chunks.

Once you have learnt to set small challenges you can start on bigger, much bigger goals, "Great Big Hairy-Assed Goals" as I once heard a coach call them. I have some nice big ones: to own a Huf Haus, have a 36ft yacht, and to set up a school for blind children! That last one is only just appearing on the horizon and I have no idea how it's going to happen yet, but I know that if I start telling people about it, I will start to find ways to make it happen!

So, go ahead, dear reader, and plan your life out in clear, well-defined terms – make pictures, put lots of sound and feelings around them, and experience the kind of life you want to lead, in as much detail as you can get!

Don't Put All Your Eggs in One Basket

The most successful people I know don't use their own money, or, at least they don't put all of their own money into one property. They are more than happy to use other people's money, which usually means that they will start off by using mortgages, and then later on borrowing from individuals or institutions. This is purely so that they are not exposing all their money to one project; if it is spread around multiple investments they can make adjustments and alterations as things change.

More is Better

I once had a potential client who had £100,000 to invest. I couldn't persuade him to use his money to build a portfolio, and he decided to buy a house in the city where his daughter was a student and make that a student house. He said that if that worked he would get another. The problem with this philosophy is that if that house went wrong for any reason he could lose a lot of money on it (not all of his money – that hardly ever happens with property, by the way, because even if the house burns down you still own the land). And, he would see it as a failure and not bother to do it again.

If he had come to me and said, "OK, Steve, how should I do it?" I could have explained to him that by using the money for deposits and getting mortgages, I could produce a cash-flowing portfolio with money that could be recycled to build a very large portfolio that would keep on growing.

Now this is what would happen if one of those houses went wrong…he buys a house for £100,000 with a mortgage of £80,000, so his deposit is just £20,000. It goes wrong for whatever reason and the house has to be sold for a discounted price of £80,000. How much has he risked and lost? Just £20,000 and he *still* has the other properties.

Now that's a very simplistic example, but the point is quite clear I think. Couple this with the gains I illustrated earlier in this chapter, and you should be able to see the advantages of a portfolio.

There are other advantages too. With maintenance, I have often had my builder working on a major refurbishment on one property and had a tenant from another one call me to say that the fence had broken, or the wind has blown some tiles off the roof. All I have to do is send the builder a text with the address and he will very happily pop round and fix it, mostly without charging me any more than the materials. If you are using a letting agent they will possibly offer you a discount for multiple properties. Insurance companies offer portfolio policies, and so on. You will also find that you can get new tenants from your existing tenants; I find that because I have tenants from eastern European countries, they recommend me to their friends and families who move to the UK.

Self-Management or Hands-Free?

Managing property takes time and effort. There are a lot of laws governing landlords now, and you need to keep up-to-date with them; falling foul of them can be very costly and could even land you in prison. You must be aware of: gas safety certificates, protecting deposits, issuing section 21s or section 8s, how to write up a legally binding Assured Shorthold Tenancy agreement, and much more.

If you still want to manage your own portfolio,

then you should join an organisation such as the Residential Landlords Association or the National Landlords Association. They will keep you up-to-date and they run courses to help you keep on the right side of the law.

There are links to both organisations on my website at www.steve-evans.org.

Using a letting agent can help to keep you on the right side of the law too, but you must check them out and don't trust them implicitly because they don't all do their job properly. Make sure they belong to a recognised trade association, make sure they are insured, and get yourself educated so that you know what they should be doing and how they should be doing it, because if ever you get taken to court it's you who will be up before the judge, not them.

Buy, Refurbish, Refinance (PROP)

P: Purchase…at a discount

You will need to learn about sold prices in your chosen area because you won't know when you're getting a bargain. It may surprise you to know that people don't always sell their house for the most amount of money they can get; they are motivated by other things, and if you can figure out what is motivating them to sell, you have a very powerful tool for negotiation.

So why do people sell at a discount? There are many reasons why someone will sell you their property for less than the going rate; here are just a few examples:

- Divorce – whether to spite their ex or just to get a quick settlement.

- Moving abroad – if they've got a job and have to start on a specific date they may not want to leave it in the hands of a third party.

- Repossession – they are in arrears and the lender is taking them to court; if you have your money in place, and you act very fast, you could land a good 'un!

- Downsizing or upsizing – they may be under pressure from others to get a move on. Again, offer them a quick sale, and you're in.

Now that you've got your discounted house, you can get on with the:

R: Refurbishment

Do not get carried away with this – it is for tenants, not you or someone buying. Quite a few of my tenants like to paint a room or two themselves, and I always let them. I said earlier that you are refurbishing for two people; the second is the valuer and for them you need to show that you have made some sort of improvement to the house. You could put in a new boiler and radiators, you might put on a conservatory, or perhaps consider investing in a new kitchen or bathroom. These are all things that could justify an increase in value for the last part of our strategy.

O: Occupy

There are many ways of getting tenants, and you should have a go at all of them at one time or another. Obviously letting agents are the first people to consult; have a talk with some and invite them around to quote. Listen carefully to all their costs as it can pretty much cost you the first month's rent when you hand it all over to them. Ask for a breakdown of all their fees as you might feel that you can do some of the work yourself and so save a bit.

You could try online agencies. I have used one in the past and found them to be very good and helpful.

Social media is becoming more and more useful. People will use it to search for places in which to live, and you can advertise on some of the sites.

P. Pull money out
Now this is where the really cool stuff happens, so concentrate – this is the bit I found quite hard to understand the first time I heard it.

Just to keep the numbers simple and easy for people like me to comprehend, we'll take a house that on the open market could sell for £100,000. The people selling it need £70,000, so you buy it from them for £70,000 and you get an 80% mortgage. This means you are borrowing £56,000 and your deposit is £14,000. Now, six months later with the house all nicely refurbished and happy tenants living in it, you've improved the house with a new kitchen and bathroom, and it's nicely decorated in plain old magnolia. You go back to your lender and ask them to send round a valuer because you feel it is now worth £100,000. The valuer agrees and you borrow 80% of that new value – £80,000.

Now let's look at what happened. You borrowed £80,000 and out of that you have paid off your first mortgage of £56,000, leaving £24,000. So, if you then take out of that the money you put in at the beginning – your deposit of £14,000 and your refurbishment costs of, say, £10,000 – what have you got left in the property? Answer – nothing! You got all your money back out of the deal, and you are left with a house that is paying you about £150-200 every month for as long as you want it! Obviously if you keep your costs for the refurbishment down or get a bigger discount, you may even make some extra cash out of it.

Remember, I have simplified the numbers for illustratiive purposes.

Demographics

Wherever you are investing, you need to work out who your typical tenants are. Broadly speaking they fall into three main types: unemployed – find out what rates the council are paying for one through four bedrooms (the government won't pay for more than four bedrooms); blue collar workers – these are your shop assistants, factory or warehouse workers, etc., and they will tend to want to pay more than the unemployed and be in slightly nicer areas; and then at the top you have your professionals – they often like living in shared houses with all the bills included in the rent, and they like high-end places with 50-inch TVs and high quality broadband.

The easiest category for our PROP model is the blue collar as they are in slightly more upmarket areas where property does sell and you can get your valuations up.

What is Value?

Everything is relative; to determine the value of anything you need comparisons. I was with a friend of a friend in Hastings once and we were looking in the window of an estate agent. The friend said, "Wow, property is cheap here". I asked her what made her say that, and she replied that a three-bedroom house around her way would cost a good £50k more. I asked her where she lived, "Oxford" she replied. Well properties would cost more; Oxford is more affluent than Hastings.

The value of anything is the price someone is willing to give you on the day you make up your mind to sell. As an investor you must decide what the right price for your strategy is. What price makes it work for you?

Yield – To determine what good value is for you,

you need a tool, a rule of thumb. Here's the one that I use all the time – multiply your month's rent by 12 to get a year's rent, divide that number by the purchase price, multiply that result by 100, and that gives you your yield in percentage terms. You should work on 8.5% as being the bottom level, as anything below that is going to lose you money. As I have said, this is a rule of thumb, there are exceptions, and when I work one-to-one with a client I can spend a lot more time getting into the detail of what is good value for them.

What Specialists are Needed?

One of the most important members of your team is your mortgage advisor, who should be someone that understands things from an investor's point of view. They should have investments of their own as well as clients who have portfolios. Your mortgage advisor should be able to source you special discounts and exclusive products; they should know the reps of the big lenders. If you don't know anyone like that, just contact me through my web page at www.steve-evans.org

Next you need a solicitor; again they should have investment property of their own and act for clients who have large portfolios. You should get them set up with your entire ID and references before you start making offers – that way there won't be any unnecessary delays that could jeopardise your purchase. Again, I will happily suggest a solicitor if you contact me.

Then, I'm afraid, it's the trades. All I can say here is, get recommendations from other landlords; do some networking, talk to others, and make sure that the tradespeople you engage know that you are part of a group of landlords. That way they should look after you and not rip you off too much.

SUMMARY

In this chapter we talked about the value of strategies – how important they are, and how they keep you focused on your goals. We also covered setting goals and how to get connected to them using all your senses. We looked at the yield calculation that makes sure you buy at the right price to make a profit, and discussed the different types of tenant – discovering which work best for the PROP strategy.

STEVE'S TOP TIPS

1. Plan a strategy…with a strategy and a plan to execute it, you can do it even with your eyes shut.

2. Avoid shiny objects…keep focused on the plan – do not deviate and you will get there.

3. Set goals…start by setting small, manageable targets, and when you've got the hang of it, set GREAT BIG HAIRY-ASSED GOALS!

4. Spread your risk…by having multiple properties and using other people's money, you will gain on the swings what you might lose on the roundabouts.

5. Manage your portfolio…learn all about managing property and tenants so that whether you DIY or employ an agent, you will keep on the right side of the law.

6. Do PROPerty PROPerly…Purchase, Refurbish, Occupy and Pull your money out by refinancing at a higher value than you bought. You might even make cash.

7. Decide who your tenants are…work out what kinds of tenants you are aiming to attract – professional, blue collar or unemployed. Make sure your property meets their expectations.

8. Refurbish…remember you are not living in it and you are not trying to sell it! Keep it simple and concentrate on improvements that will get the value up.

HUNTING FOR BARGAINS

WHY DO YOU NEED A BARGAIN?

To Create Value

What I love about looking for discounted property is that it can be done in any market; whether it's an up-market or a down-market, there are always people who can't sell or who need to sell fast. As an investor, you should be looking to make money when you buy. What does that mean? Let's just keep using the nice round number of £100,000 (that's not for you, it's for me, so that I can do the maths!) You need to buy the house that is worth £100,000 for £80,000 or less; that way, if that is a house that could easily sell for £100,000 then you have £20,000 of what's termed instant equity – you've effectively gained £20,000 as soon as you've bought.

To Find the Hidden Treasure

Naturally you are not going to find a house below market value straight away. It takes a lot of looking. It's not about going into an estate agent and saying, "Give me one of those bargains the investors get". Remember, an agent's job is to get the best price they can for their client, so don't aggravate them. You have to bide your time; you'll need to look at dozens and dozens of houses, including some that don't match your criteria, in order to spot the deal. Remember, this is a deal that could net you £20,000 or £30,000, so isn't that worth waiting for?

You will have to try different sourcing techniques, such as leafleting, newspaper ads, and networking.

Even when you find something to make an offer on, it might not come off the first time you offer on it; it could be after the third time of asking that you get accepted, and that can take months of patient work. Keep all this in mind and make multiple offers, and make sure you keep track of them! Keep a spreadsheet so that you know what you offered and when. Patience is the name of the game here – you will have to put in a lot of footwork, and do lots and lots of viewings before you find your first bargain.

To Reuse Your Capital

Keep in mind the ultimate goal. That is to find some way you can create up-lift in the value of the property. Once you have bought at your discount, you then create extra value by putting in a new bathroom and/or kitchen, replacing the heating system, or perhaps extending somewhere. After six months, you can go back to your lender and ask to have the property revalued in order to get your money back out, and maybe even make a bit of extra cash. Once you have done that you can start the next project. Warning: don't spend that extra money on a new toy for yourself; the tax man may stop you claiming the cost of borrowing against your income. This is where having an accountant who understands property investing is very important.

WHAT YOU SHOULD KNOW

Definition of a Bargain

A bargain is something you can buy for less than someone else will pay. A good example of bargains can be seen at auction houses where you can buy a property for a very good price, and then sell it on later for £20,000 or £30,000 more than you paid.

Have you ever known someone who is in a hurry to get shot of something? Maybe they are going abroad and need to sell their car, so they've let it go for a couple of hundred less than you've seen that same make and model go for on eBay, or in your local papers. You will only know that something is a bargain when you have an intimate knowledge of your market, and you will only have that knowledge when you live it, sleep it, and breathe it. You must become an expert in your chosen area; get to know what every road is like, and what every type of house tends to sell for.

In other words, you'll only know if something is a bargain when you have a comparable – something else exactly the same, or very close to, the thing you are interested in buying.

Methods of Research

You can save yourself a massive amount of time and shoe leather by getting to know some websites.

The market leader and reference point for most people in the industry is Rightmove: www. rightmove.co.uk.

Set up a free account so that you can bookmark

properties you are interested in. You can even set up alerts so that it will email you when something comes on the market that fits your criteria. You will also find comprehensive information on sold prices – these are very important to you because they tell you the value of everything in your area.

Another very good and comprehensive site is Zoopla: www.zoopla.co.uk.

Zoopla has a very useful tool for working out potential value; you just give it the postal address of your property, and then you can fill in extras that the property might have, e.g. double glazing or central heating. If your house doesn't have them and you want to know if it's worth putting them in, just fill them in on the form and it will give you an idea of what that would make the house worth.

HOW TO FIND BELOW POTENTIAL VALUE PROPERTIES

Estate agents are not the only source of property. There are many and varied reasons why people will sell to you at below potential value prices, and when you are aware of them you will start to spot bargains all over the place. Listen to conversations in coffee shops, bars and cafes; you will hear people talking about issues that can lead you to their needing to sell a house for one reason or another.

People who need to sell quickly need to know you're out there, so you need to find ways to contact them. Leafleting, advertising and getting yourself known as someone who buys quickly and helpfully are all things you need to try your hand at until you find the one that you like. Once you have found the method that best suits you and your target area, do more of it!

Problems that lead to a bargain…

- Repossession: the owners cannot keep up their repayments, and the bank has applied to the courts to get possession of the property and get them thrown out.

- Divorce: the owners have to sell in order to go their separate ways.

- Moving abroad: the owners have a job that starts by a certain date and they need to be there, with the money in the bank, in order to start their new life.

- Changing job and location: same as moving abroad but staying in the UK, and trying to do it all themselves instead of using agents.

- Upsizing: there's a baby on the way and there's no room for them – another deadline that can't be put off!

- Downsizing: the house is getting too much to manage, either because the owners are getting older, the children have flown the nest, or they can't afford it anymore.

Estate agents won't necessarily know or, even when they are aware, tell you about these issues, so you have to find them some other way. I have found leafleting to be a pretty good way of getting to the people I want to talk to. It is time consuming and can be hard to manage through a third party, but I think it is worth the effort. Your options are: do it yourself – very time consuming but reliable; pay an agency – hard to know if your leaflets are being delivered; put them into a local free paper – they tend to fall out or get thrown away with all the others; or team up with someone else who wants to put leaflets through doors, like a local takeaway.

Newspaper ads are quite effective. I find in my area that people are still reading their local paper and property issues are quite a hot topic; obviously this one comes at quite a price, but again you are after a pretty big fish and you need the right bait.

If you're good with IT, then building a website to capture leads could work, although you are up against some fairly tough competition. There are some well-designed national sites that have very big money behind them, so you should go very local, and make your site show you are a real person who is local and so understands local issues, particularly ones related to property.

If you don't live in the area but you want people to think you do, you can get a phone number that uses that area code and is forwarded to wherever you like. You can divert it to your mobile or a landline of your choice. However, I find that most people these days are happy to call another mobile because it's included in their call plan.

Estate agents can be an excellent source of bargains when you handle them with care. The trick with them is to build a really good rapport. The way to get on with them is to remember that the people who pay them are the sellers, so their obligation is to them. Having said that, they also need to sell and that is where you can take advantage of your value to them. Let your agent know that you are in the market for more than one property, tell them that you can buy quickly (be sure that you can), and be realistic with your offers (don't insult their intelligence). If you ever see a property that works for you because the asking price makes the gross yield 8.5% or above, it is 20% below its potential value and you can create up-lift of at least £10,000; the sensible thing to do is to offer the full asking price. This will earn you far more brownie points than being greedy and trying to get an even bigger discount. Make your agent happy, build trust and reliability with them, and they will call you when the next good deal comes along.

Specify Your Bargain

Given that you've taken all the previous steps and you are now spotting bargains everywhere, you now need to think about your strategy and which type of property fits it. Are you looking for small terraced houses for single lets that families might live in for years, where you can rely on £150-200 every month in profit? Or are you after that eight-bed HMO (House of Multiple Occupancy) that potentially provides you with £800 profit every month? Or is something in between for you?

The way to choose is to look at: who your target tenants are, what sort of housing stock there is, how much you can buy that property for, and how much you can rent it for. A useful tool for working the figures out is the yield calculation:

Calculate your gross yield…this is the rough figure that tells you whether your chosen house is the one.

For example, the house price is £95,000, and the rental value £600 per month; multiply the rent by 12 (months), which equals £7,200. Divide the result by the price of the house -£95,000 into £7,200, which equals 0.076. Now multiply that figure by 100, giving you 7.6%. This is your gross yield and is slightly below the golden figure of 8.5% gross yield. 8.5% gross yield is the point at which you should be making a profit, and so you need to consider other factors. When I have a client who comes to me with a potential deal like the example, I would then get them to look at other factors to determine whether it was a deal worth making an offer on.

Let's now look at the property – the actual bricks

and mortar. How much is it worth? This is where you need to be excellent at your research: what other similar properties nearby are on the market? How much are they asking? How much have they sold for in the last two to three years? Don't go any further back than that because you are bringing in too many other factors that influence the market, such as the economy, changes in stamp duty thresholds, or death duties.

Once you've established your property's market value and how much discount you think you can get it for, look at any potential up-lift there might be. Can you fit another bedroom in? The UK is quite different to other housing markets in that we value property primarily on the number of bedrooms. Most other property markets around the world, and all commercial property in the UK, work on square footage or meterage. So, if you can feasibly get an extra bedroom in without compromising the space in another room, then you could increase the value quite considerably. One very easy way to do this is where there is a garage. Very few people use a garage to keep their car in now. When my wife and I were looking for our home recently, we were amazed that well over 95% of the properties with garages did not have a single vehicle in them – most were utility and junk rooms! Getting these turned into extra rooms is very simple and inexpensive. You could also consider doing a loft conversion. Make sure that it would gain you an extra bedroom, and that the cost is less than the extra value it would make you.

Does your potential bargain have decent central heating or are the radiators and boiler very old? I am amazed at the age of some boilers. Remember that you'll need an EPC (Energy Performance Certificate), so having a good modern boiler can help to get your score up. The government are putting pressure on property owners, and in particular landlords, to improve the energy efficiency of their properties. It is likely that in the near future you will not be able to rent out property that has a score of F or below, so you should consider issues of energy efficiency as adding to the value.

What condition is the bathroom or kitchen in? You can get reasonably cheap, good, durable suites for a modest cost, and a new suite always makes a good impression, whether to potential tenants or to the next valuer. You can often create more space when you plan out either of these rooms carefully.

A word of caution…if you think the house could stand extending, remember you may need to get planning permission. This could take months, in some cases more than a year, and this will eat into your returns – all the time you are waiting the house is costing you money.

Compiling a Large List

If you're not computer-savvy, I suggest you face up to it and get yourself enrolled in some basic classes. By far the easiest way to keep up with your viewings is to create a spreadsheet – it's so easy to adjust, keep track of appointments, and refer back to. Keep a sheet that has the following headings:

- Postcode

- House name or number

- Street name

- Town

- Estate agent

- The name of the agent you're dealing with

- Telephone number of agent

- Date of viewing 1

- Date of viewing 2

- Made offer (yes/no)

- Offer accepted (yes/no)

Mine goes into more detail than that, but that should get you started with a database that will keep you on track.

Capturing all that information is vital for future reference – by keeping track of postcodes and street names you can see which have the most movement. As your database grows, you can put sold prices alongside the asking prices – an invaluable tool for knowing your market. Keep your notes on this spreadsheet so that when you have your offer accepted you will know why you made it in the first place. Believe me, you will sometimes have an offer accepted and think to yourself, "Why did I offer on that one?"

Selecting the Best One

Whether you're buying for yourself or investing, every house has its good and bad points so you need to set out a list of criteria. My wife and I recently moved home, and we had an extensive list of wants and not-wants which included: quiet road, preferably cul-de-sac, because we have cats; minimum master bedroom size; our own drive, because I don't like going onto the street and trying to find our car amongst all the others (don't panic, I don't try to drive it, just unload shopping etc.!); and many more personal likes and dislikes. You should do the same – not as personal as mine, but you need to think about the sorts of things your tenants might be concerned about (which won't be the same as yours). For example, a tenant might like to be on a main road close to local shops and have a bus stop outside their door; I know I would have loved that in my piano tuning days when I had to get a bus virtually every time I went out.

Once you have selected the properties that most closely match your criteria, go ahead and make your offer and remember, "No" means *"Not now"*, not *"Never"*. Keep a record of what you offered and when, so that when the agent comes back to you in three months and says that the house is back on the market, you can just look up the address on your spreadsheet and let them know that you are still in the market for it.

SUMMARY

In this chapter I have kept your mind on the issue of value. I explained that the value of anything is how much someone who wants to buy is prepared to pay at the time someone else needs to sell. I explained that you are going to need to do a lot of hunting before you find your first bargain. It wasn't all bad news though, because I taught you how to spot the people who need to sell at a discount. I explained that there are people who have other criteria besides getting the highest price – people who sell for many other reasons not related to price at all. You read all about the different ways you can find the sellers that don't go to agents, get in ahead of the agents and offer a quick sale. You also learnt about all the different ways of up-lifting the value of your property and you got my favourite calculation, the yield calculator – the way to work out very quickly in your head how much you should buy the house for. Lastly, I gave you a basic spreadsheet list of headings – you should make sure you use a spreadsheet because it will build into a comprehensive record of property values in your area.

STEVE'S TOP TIPS

1. Viewing: you should be prepared to view at least 50 properties before you find one that could work.

2. Estate agents: an excellent source of potential bargains – you just need to spend time building rapport and trust with them. Remember, they are obligated to the vendor, not you.

3. Getting rapport with agents: remember that they are supposed to be getting the best price possible for the vendor. Get to know them as an individual. Buy them lunch or just a coffee occasionally. Offer them a lift to save them petrol.

4. Sourcing deals: newspaper ads. These can cost a bit but do go direct to sellers.

5. Leaflets: If you do them yourself it is time consuming. If you pay others it is difficult to control.

6. Networking: there are many and varied groups, all of which are worth a try so you can see which one you find the most helpful.

7. Bargains: to find a bargain you need to know your market. Get excellent knowledge of your investment area, find out what sells and at what price. A bargain is something you can buy at a price that is well below what you absolutely know you can sell it for.

8. Creating up-lift: you can do this in a number of ways – upgrading the bathroom and/or kitchen; creating an extra room (e.g. turning a garage into a bedroom); upgrading anything connected to energy efficiency; or putting an extension on the property.

9. Remortgaging: when you buy with a mortgage, you are usually forced to wait six months before your lender will let you remortgage.

10. Research and valuations: the two best sites for finding values and learning about market movement are: www.rightmove.co.uk and www.zoopla.co.uk

ACQUIRING LONG-TERM ASSETS

WHY BUY & REFURBISH?

There are many strategies out there these days that teach us how to control assets (or in our case, properties) without owning them. The biggest problem with these clever and very worthwhile techniques is that, for our purposes, they are not building us a portfolio that we have long-term control over. My overwhelming concern is that I help people who would otherwise be faced with an uncertain future of working beyond 70 years old, and suffering declining income and living standards.

TO GAIN CONTROL OF THE ASSET

By owning your portfolio you will have complete

control. It will be up to you how much you leverage it financially. That is, how much you borrow against the property in the future. If you decide to sell any or all of it, you can – although I would strongly advise against selling, ever! Most experts in this industry agree that you should borrow up to 75% of the total value of your portfolio. By borrowing against your property you are reducing the inheritance tax bill you leave your beneficiaries.

Let's just think about the whole subject of borrowing for a moment. There is a huge distinction between borrowing against your own home and borrowing against your cash-flowing portfolio. There is nothing better than living in a home that is paid for. I know because I do, thanks to my investments. When it comes to your investments, it's a different matter. You are entitled to claim the cost of borrowing against the income from your property. That means that the interest on your mortgages is an allowable expense. If you pay down your loans, you will end up paying more tax! Remember, property goes up in value every eight to ten years, so you can keep on borrowing up to 75% of that value as it increases. That means that you can pull cash out of it every time the value goes up; this is the key to our strategy.

Just coming back to succession, imagine you have a portfolio worth £1,500,000, you've paid off all the mortgages, and it is generating £70,000 rent every year. When you die, your beneficiaries will have to pay inheritance tax and income tax at whatever rate they happen to be at that time. That is the sort of scenario that brought down the landed gentry in the early 20th century; so many properties had to be sold just to pay inheritance tax! At the time of writing, this tax has to be paid within six months of your death; that puts a lot of pressure on the executors to get everything sorted out. If they don't do this in time, HMRC will charge them interest.

So, buy your property at a discount (at least 20%), borrow someone else's money to pay for about 75% of its value, and keep borrowing against that value as it increases over time.

There is one last concept I want you to get your head around – this one took me a long time to understand, so don't expect it to make total sense the first time you read it.

History clearly tells us that property ALLWAYS goes up in value. In fact, I have seen charts that show this growth since Domesday. Did you know that when the Domesday Book was written, the total value of all property and land in the UK was only worth about £1,000,000? I bet that, like me, you know at least one person who owns one property that is worth three times that. If you've read this book from the beginning, you will know that the first property I bought cost me the princely sum of £34,000 and I put down £12,000 as my deposit, leaving me with £22,000 to pay. If I'd used an interest only mortgage and stayed in that little flat for 25 years, I would have had a bill of £22,000 to pay and my flat would have been worth £365,000. In other words, inflation over 30 years would have obliterated my debt.

To Create Value

The key to the strategy in this book is creating value or up-lift. When you are viewing and offering, the questions you must have uppermost in your mind are "How can I make this property worth more? How can I add value?", and so when it comes to refurbishing you should have a plan in mind, and get started on it immediately after you take possession.

There are some important areas that will improve the value of property. The first is to get light, air, and a perception of space. It doesn't cost very much, for example, to knock down the dividing wall between a kitchen and rear reception room (make sure you get professional advice from your surveyor or structural engineer). Treat any damp issues; I prefer to get my builder to treat the plaster directly where possible, but there are ventilation systems available too.

When you are going for the second round of finance in our PROP model, (P – pull cash out), the valuer will want to know what you've done to improve the house. It's a good idea to be there when they visit, and just very gently point out the great stuff you have done. They are not all that impressed when it looks like all you have done is give it a lick of paint. Show them things like: a new boiler, nice new bathroom, a good quality kitchen, and decent external windows and doors.

To Make it Easily Lettable

There is a world of difference between decorating your own home and refurbishing a property to let. With rental property, you need to think about functionality, accessibility, and simplicity, whilst at the same time keeping your mind on the revaluation. There's no point in putting colour anywhere, as whatever you do the tenants won't like it. Keep colours plain and simple. It's a bit of a cliché, but magnolia for the walls with white ceilings and biscuit-coloured carpets will do just fine. I sometimes get tenants asking if they can paint a wall here or there, and I always say yes, providing that they don't use a revolting colour like black or dark brown that would show through later when they leave.

ACQUIRING A PROPERTY

Follow a System

Whether you are going direct to vendor or, perhaps even more importantly, when dealing with an estate agent, you must be able to move fast if you're going to get that deal. It's no good offering to buy a property quickly if you don't have your team ready to go as soon as your offer is accepted. So, make sure your mortgage advisor knows: what kind of property you are buying, what rent you expect to get, how much you are buying it for, what size loan you require, which product is best, and more. Have a solicitor ready to go too; they are notorious for not rushing no matter how much you need them to. When your mortgage broker has everything they need, they can provide you with a DIP, or Decision in Principle; that is a document you can give the estate agent that shows them you can get the loan. Remember that in the case of both professions, you should seek out someone who has investment property themselves or have clients who have portfolios. They will be much more sympathetic to your needs.

Your professional representatives will need to verify your identity, so have ID papers ready, such as your passport, driving licence, and up-to-date utility bills and bank statements. By having all this ready, you will be able to go through the process of buying very quickly and efficiently.

I can provide the contact details of competent people. So if you need any help finding suitable professionals you can contact me at www.steve-evans.org

Negotiation

I know, I know, I know. When you're buying your first property it's really exciting. I get that because it was for me too. I think I lost out in terms of getting deals with the first couple of purchases because I was excited and didn't keep cool when negotiating the price. Keep in mind that there are an awful lot of chimneys out there, and if you don't get this one, there's another one with your name on it. Really, this is a wide open marketplace and you will get that deal! Remember that you are the answer to the vendor's problems. I'm not saying that you need to be hardnosed and heartless, but just make sure that your figures aren't compromised, because that will affect your income in the future.

When negotiating with anybody, it is important to make sure you let them do the majority of the talking. Keep quiet until you're ready to show your hand. Remember, you have one mouth and two ears – use them in that ratio. When you are in front of a vendor and there is no agent involved, ask questions like: "How soon do you need to leave?", "What's your reason for selling?", and "How much do you need to clear your debts?" Always ask open questions where possible. Open questions are questions that start with a Wh or an H such as who, what, where, when and how. These questions invoke a detailed response rather than a closed question like, "Did you come on the train?" A closed question will tend to generate a one word answer, like "Yes" or "No".

When you're dealing with an estate agent, it's worth being a little more forthright – I don't mean loud and brash, just gently let them know how well-placed you are to buy quickly. Mention that you have your mortgage ready to go and that your solicitor is very good at quick responses. Also let your agent know that you are in the market for more than one property, but that they need to be at the right price and in the right area. Use vague, non-specific statements: "I'm looking for one, two, or three-bed properties". "I'd offer something in the region of the 80s or 90s". Neuro Linguistic Programming (NLP) refers to this as being artfully vague.

Financing

Earlier I talked about a potential client who had £100,000 to invest. I showed you how, by purchasing several properties with that money he would have: spread his risk, recycled deposits, and multiplied the gains in equity every time property went up in value. Let's look into those concepts in a bit more detail.

Leverage – this is important! The banks know that property is an excellent investment. There is no other business that they will lend on at the same levels. You can get buy to let mortgages at 75% all day long. That means that you only have to risk investing at 25% every time you buy a property. So, you buy a house for £100,000, and you put £25,000 down. The house then climbs 10% in value, thus making it worth £110,000. The return on your £25,000 investment is £10,000. The bank has invested £75,000. Now, just look at what happens for them…they, the bank, make their money by charging you interest; therefore, the bank only cares about you paying that interest on the £75,000 over the next 20 to 25 years. The bank makes nothing from the increase in equity and it makes nothing from the rent. You, on the other hand, get capital appreciation plus income from the rent!

Now here's the view from the other side of the coin. You pay £100,000 cash for the same house; it goes up 10%, making it worth £110,000. Okay, so in this scenario you gain 10% on your investment, but to get that 10% you've risked all of your money for a 10% gain, and in the other scenario you only risked £25,000 and you got a cool 50% gain. Not only that, you did it five times! With this approach your £100,000 has made you £50,000. Now that's what I call investing!

I know these are simplistic numbers but it's the principle that matters.

Leverage just means that you are using someone else's money in order to make your money go further. You are borrowing at 5% or maybe 10%, whatever rate the banks set at the time so that you can make 40% or 50% on the money you put in. Believe me, get this concept clear in your mind and you will be well on your way to success!

REFURBISHING A PROPERTY

Consider Costs v Benefits

It is definitely worth me repeating this advice: do not refurbish as if this were your own home. The two people you need to impress are your tenant and the valuer from the lenders. For the tenant the house should be perfectly plain and simple. There should be clean, bright walls and inoffensive patterned carpets or hard floors. Patterns on the floors disguise stains and plain coloured walls don't put off people who have strong feelings about this colour or that.

Your tradespeople will want to do things perfectly, and so they should. You need to work out just how much you really need to do. When you are dealing with electricity, gas or water obviously there are issues of safety and law that must be observed. The harder decisions are around plastering and finishes. It's very nice to have freshly plastered flat and perfectly smooth walls but trust me, the tenants don't notice them. Only plaster where you have damp that needs dealing with or where the walls are crumbling when you strip the paper off. Internal doors are quite cheap to replace, or you can get them dipped and freshly painted. This can make a big difference for not very much cost.

With kitchens and bathrooms you should look at keeping what's there so long as it is serviceable, and just replace the things that make the biggest impact. For example: check out the carcasses in the kitchen – if they are solid enough just change the doors and drawer fronts. Taps can tend to be expensive so consider keeping them if they are serviceable and just change the bathroom suite or, if the suite is okay but the taps are chipped and worn, just change them and the whole room will look better.

Always look at the end goal. How much can you rent this house for? By spending that extra bit of cash will it really earn you that much more?

Use Other People's Time

Everybody gets tempted to DIY…don't. I know you think you're saving money, but you're not.

Back in my piano tuning days I occasionally came across a music teacher, often the head of the music department in large secondary schools, who knew most of the theory and who would try to save the school's money by attempting to tune their own pianos. They never had any major catastrophes but they didn't get it perfect either. They often caused the tuning pins to become loose, and that meant that the piano didn't stay in tune as well as it should have. The thing is that if you occasionally fit radiators and pipes together, for example, you will get it done but it will have taken you three or four times as long as a plumber who does it all day every day. The professionals get things done quickly and accurately. That head of music may have saved the cost of getting me out to tune a piano, but it will have taken them three or four hours against my one hour.

Your time is valuable too. If you spend days, weeks and months working on a project you are not out talking to estate agents and looking around at other potential deals for the future. When you have spent time building relationships with agents and then go and get stuck into a refurbishment project the agents will forget you. If the agents don't think you're out looking for deals they will pass them on to someone else.

Raise Finance

For those who really love to use other people's money or whose budgets are squeezed, there are a couple of ways you can raise the money for the refurbish. The first is refurbishment mortgage. The lender will lend you enough to get the project started and then you have to achieve certain goals in specific time frames in order to release the next block of money. The problem with this type of mortgage is that you have to achieve your goals within very specific time constraints.

A second and very popular way of funding the refurbishment is to borrow from a friend or family member. This method works well because people with money in the bank are frustrated with the lack of interest they can get. The really great thing for you is that, should the project get delayed for any reason, you can go back to them and explain why they won't be getting their money back for a little bit longer. As they are usually someone you know quite well it is possible to renegotiate longer terms with them.

There are many different ways of setting up a loan agreement with someone, and it all depends on the relationship you have with them. My favourite is called the roll-up method. At the time of writing, most of my peers offer around 10% spread over six or 12 months, approximately 1% a month. Roll-up simply means that we don't pay the interest until the end of the period. Example, I borrow £30,000 from you for 12 months at 10%, and at the end of 12 months I give you back £30,000 plus your interest of £3,000. The advantage for me is that if I finish my project early I can pay you back early and there are no early redemption penalties.

SUMMARY

This chapter has looked at the long-term plan in my strategy. You read about borrowing 75% of the value of your portfolio being the standard level for the investing industry, and this means that you will reduce your income tax and your beneficiaries' inheritance tax when you're gone. I explained how inflation can wipe out debt. You learnt that you can create value by buying at a discount, extending or converting to create extra bedrooms, or replacing things like kitchens/bathrooms or putting in a new central heating system. I also explained that decorating for tenants should be done simply and with plain magnolia-like colours, and you learnt that it's okay to let tenants paint the odd wall themselves. When it comes to purchasing your property I told you that you must have your paperwork ready and everything in place such as your ID for solicitors and mortgage brokers alike. With regard to negotiations I pointed out that you must keep as quiet as possible and find out as much as possible before declaring your hand. You learnt that you should use your ears and mouth in proportion to each other – in other words, use your ears twice as much as your mouth. You learnt that open questions are the most effective to use when finding out something – open questions are questions that begin with W or H, such as who, what, where and when. On the subject of finance I illustrated the power of leverage to explain how with a 25% deposit on £100,000 investment you will make a 50% return when the property's value goes up by 10%.

STEVE'S TOP TIPS

1. Buy and hold – never, ever sell your property!

2. Borrowing keeps your income tax bill down.

3. Borrowing keeps your beneficiaries' inheritance tax bill down.

4. Get your own home paid for and build debt on your portfolio.

5. Inflation negates property debt.

6. To get tenants, keep colours plain and for valuers, show real improvements like replacing: boiler, kitchen, bathroom and windows/doors.

7. Get a great team around you.

8. Find a mortgage advisor who has property investments themselves.

9. Make sure your solicitor has a portfolio or has clients who have.

10. Have ID documents verified with the professionals so that there are no delays when your offer is accepted.

11. When negotiating use open questions: what, when, how, where and who.

12. You have one mouth and two ears, use in that proportion.

13. Think about what and who you can leverage in order to do whatever it is that you do best.

GENERATING INCOME

LETTING

The UK's population has undergone a paradigm shift during the early 21st century. Prior to the 1990s the vast majority of the working population aspired to own their own property by the time they reached their 30s or before. As I write, we are rapidly approaching 20% of the UK population renting and that figure is predicted to keep rising. The average age of a first time buyer is close to 40, and most students now don't expect to buy their home in the foreseeable future.

This is all fantastic news for those of us who want to invest in property because it proves that there is an endless supply of tenants, and tenants are what keep investments cashflowing. In fact, it has been my experience that this is usually where investing abroad falls down. There are not enough tenants who want to live in the new buildings you are funding to build.

Rent - Costs = Cashflow

It is worth me repeating the yield formula I use when I'm deciding on a price for an investment property.

YIELD – a rough calculation of gross yield is rent multiplied by 12, divided by purchase price, multiplied by 100.

You should be looking for a result of 8.5% or higher to be certain that you will make money every month.

Other than paying the mortgage, there are many more costs associated with running a property portfolio and you must make sure from the outset that you will be able to cover them and make your profit.

Lenders' Requirements

The key to everything I have said and everything I am going to say in this book is getting tenants to pay your costs and make you money! I am not alone in this; the lenders will judge your purchase on what they think you can rent it for and how strong that rental market is. The institutions all require that the rent is at least 125% of the monthly mortgage repayments – this is, in my opinion, the barest minimum and should not be used as a measure of whether or not you have bagged a good deal.

Knowing All the Costs

People spend a lot of time thinking about the financing of their property and forget that there are other expenses to consider. You must be aware of all the costs related to your investments in order to know whether or not you are making money. Otherwise you will find out the hard way, usually too far down the road to do anything about it and you may have to sell. By knowing all of your expenses you can take decisions on cutting costs if you find you are not making enough profit.

Cashflow v Capital Growth

When I was based in London and just starting out in the world of property, everybody talked about capital. All the people who responded to my leaflets looking for those who were stuck and unable to sell believed that they had equity. The truth at that time however was very different. Prices did not move for at least four years, and it wasn't until about six years later that things started to move significantly again. I viewed a lot of properties that were owned by investors who were losing money because they were not getting the capital growth they had banked on!

Before the banking crisis in 2008 I actually heard professional investors saying that they were funding investments and waiting for capital growth. What they meant was that they were subsidising their mortgage out of their own pockets because the cost of the loan was more than the rent they were getting. I don't see those people on the circuit now, and I expect that is because they had to sell due to property prices not going up and therefore them not getting the capital growth they were betting on. Yes, that's right, I said betting, because investing and waiting for capital growth is not, in my opinion, investing – it is gambling.

What we are about is investing for income, and for income we need tenants. Your tenants should pay your mortgage, your insurance and all the other costs associated with purchasing and running your property, and you should get at least £150 a month clear cash after everything is taken out. A couple of my properties make me £300 every month and my small HMOs (Houses of Multiple Occupancy) produce upwards of £700 every month.

WHAT YOU NEED TO KNOW

Warning!

When advertising a vacancy you must: explain any charges or fees attached to applying for the tenancy and you must have an EPC (Energy Performance Certificate).

The law also requires you to hold a gas safety certificate and it must be renewed every year.

NEVER, EVER hand over your keys to potential tenants until you have:

- A signed tenancy agreement

- The deposit

- The first month's rent

Finding Tenants

Broadly speaking there are three types of tenant: unemployed, student and professional. Within the student and professional categories there are some subcategories. In the case of students there are your standard grant-maintained students who are looking for affordable accommodation. As well as these, there are students from overseas who can afford more expensive property. I won't dwell on students other than to say that they can work in some places, but you do need to get expert advice and definitely find an agent as keeping the rent tracked and up-to-date requires good record keeping.

Unemployed tenants can be a great strategy for those who are good at studying the system and taking full advantage of the fact that the government need landlords to accommodate them. Personally I don't have the patience to learn all the rules and do the paperwork, and the margins are very tight.

The professionals are the tenants that suit our strategy best, so let's look at them in a little more detail. Blue collar workers are shop assistants, factory/warehouse workers and so on. These are good tenants for me and I can house them all day long. Next there are post-graduate young professionals, which are good for filling HMOs, and lastly there are family professionals, another field altogether.

What your tenants want in a home and what you want in your home can often be completely different. Families will be looking for schools and convenient shopping; they may also want to be near public transport, doctors and dentists. In short, they are best suited to the outskirts of towns.

Single young professionals like living in shared houses. They love to have all that the town has to offer right there on the doorstep. A young professional will be very happy to have a couple of take-away restaurants within five minutes' walk. The station and night buses are highly desirable too. They are much happier if they only have one bill every month – your rent. That means you have to take care of everything else: gas, electricity, water and even the council tax. They will expect good broadband and Sky TV. Get all these things right and you are onto a winner!

Selecting Tenants

Never judge a book by its cover. So you think you're a good judge of character? Choosing the right tenant is not an exact science. The only real way to get good at it is to do it until you get it right, but there are a few things you can consider looking out for. I think every new landlord goes through what

I experienced, and that is the worry of not getting a tenant. Don't. There are hundreds of tenants out there; you just haven't got enough noise going on on the grapevine yet. The most important thing to remember when you are looking for tenants is that this is your house they are getting access to, and you only have total control before you let it. So be fussy and be very careful. Most of all be mindful that this is a business you are running, not a charity.

Once you have signed it over to a tenant they have many more rights than you in the eyes of the law and you must respect it and work with it. Laws have evolved to protect tenants against bad landlords, and I for one respect that. I have heard some really bad stories of very unreasonable landlords who just treat their tenants with no respect and very little dignity. There is no need for this kind of behaviour and hopefully these laws will weed out the bad landlords and we will get a better press.

Removing Tenants

Occasionally you are going to get tenants who will misbehave – it's just the way of the world, and this is when you need the law on your side. Provided that you do things correctly the judge will rule in your favour, and in fact, when you issue the correct paperwork in the right order and get all the i's dotted and the t's crossed, the judge has no choice but to grant you possession. There is even a procedure to evict a tenant if they have behaved unlawfully within the initial fixed period of the tenancy. So, as with so much in life, get yourself educated or use someone who knows what they are doing and you will have no problems that can't be ironed out.

Contracts

There are only a couple of contracts available to landlords, and of those only one is really worth talking about in any detail. You will come across licences with some multi-let landlords and there are specific contracts for live-in landlords, but other than that the only contract you need to be aware of as a landlord of a property you don't live in is called an Assured Shorthold Tenancy agreement. The best way to get one that will stand up in court is to join a professional landlord's association. You will find a link that you can follow to the most recognised organisations, if you visit me at www. steve-evans.org

HOW TO FIND & SELECT TENANTS

Finding Tenants

Finding your tenants can be time consuming and frustrating so if you don't have loads of time on your hands I recommend using an agent. Even if you feel you can do it yourself, you should consult with local agents to get a feel for the rental values in your area. Agents offer several ways of working with you, so talk to them and see what suits you best.

When using an agent you must make sure they are members of a professional organisation that guarantees their standards of service. There have been some very bad cases of agencies becoming bankrupt and agents running off with tens of thousands of pounds of tenants' deposits and, if that happens to you as a landlord, you will be held liable for the loss. Properly insured agents who hold client accounts are essential. Visit my website for up-to-date information on which organisations you should be looking for at www.steve-evans.org

When choosing your letting agent think about the ongoing management of your property and tenants. Will you be managing them yourself or do you want the agent to do all the work and just get your money every month? Or, do you want the agent to just get you people who are interested and let you deal with the rest? The agents will offer you a mind boggling range of prices for the services they offer and it is up to you to figure it out.

Doing it yourself is a way of saving money but it is like all things you can leverage; you will need to give it a lot of time especially in the beginning when you are learning. There are websites you can advertise your property on, or I find where I am based there are still people who read the local newspaper. You could try putting a card on a notice board in your local DIY store or newsagent. I find that putting a notice in the window of the property is quite effective because it attracts the attention of people who are living in that area and who just want to live in a better or bigger house.

Selecting Tenants

You must put your tenants through a process of application and vetting. These things are worth knowing even if you intend to use an agent. Remember, once you sign the AST (Assured Shorthold Tenancy) agreement and give them your keys they can refuse to let you into your property and may not pay you any rent so get things right from the outset. Don't worry, there are lots of organisations that can help and I can lead you to them from my website: www.steve-evans.org

All you need to do is get the applicant's full name and their address details for the past three years, and the agencies will do all the footwork for you.

From time to time, you will get people who will offer to give you cash for the first month's rent plus the deposit for a quick move in with out all the vetting. DO NOT GIVE IN TO THEM! You may not get any more rent for the next six months or more. Don't even let tenants have the keys to move stuff in before the agreement date.

Now let's look at the good things to look out for. Do your applicants turn up on time? Do their clothes show that they are likely to be able to afford the rent? Are they happy to give you references? Can they prove that they have been working regularly?

Removing Tenants

You will always meet people who are very happy to bang on about how terrible tenants are and how hard it was to get rid of some evil people who were put on this earth just to make their lives miserable.

Just ignore them and listen to those of us who are dealing with tenants all the time. They are not so bad. Most tenants are just ordinary people trying to get through life as best they can. Having said that, occasionally you will get someone who doesn't play the game by the rules and for them we have systems and procedures. Get them right and the law will work fine for you.

There are two basic ways you can ask the court to grant you possession. They are known as a section 21 and a section 8. The section 21 is the most commonly used, and when done properly will work perfectly well. You just need to be patient and do things correctly; don't give the judge any reason to stall or stop it in its tracks. The basic principle of a section 21 is that the tenancy agreement should not be in the fixed period and that the tenant must have a full month's notice. Get this right and you don't have to give a reason – you can just do it to get the property back.

The section 8 is different and more complex because it is designed for the more troublesome tenants, the ones who do make your life more challenging. You can issue these during the fixed term but you have to have a very good reason and you must attend a hearing. There are many parts to a section 8 and I'm not going to go into them here. To find out more about how to submit either eviction procedure visit me at www.steve-evans.org

I always serve a post-dated section 21 on my tenants at the beginning of the tenancy so that should I need to evict them I can do it at the earliest opportunity. There's nothing wrong with doing this and it serves to warn the tenants that if they do anything like fall behind on the rent or cause trouble they will be removed at my earliest convenience. I've not yet had to evict anybody.

Contracts

Are you a details person or do you just like to leave all that to the professionals? I tend not to want to be bothered about all the detail, but since I've been a landlord and investor I've become more interested and concerned because the devil is in the detail. However, there has been considerable pressure over the years to make tenancy agreements easy to understand for the tenants. Therefore they are pretty standard and simple to follow. You can still put in your own clauses and addendums, but I wouldn't recommend straying from the accepted principles of a standard AST if I were you. Contracts are not necessarily enforceable unless they stay within the bounds of the law of the land. That is to say that only that which is contained within written laws and where precedents have been set is enforceable.

To get helpful guidance and links to high quality ASTs, visit my website at www.steve-evans.org

Voids are unavoidable when renting property. Please don't get hung up on them. Here comes some mindset stuff.

Be careful about what you concentrate on. It might well happen. Expert golfers do not focus on the bunkers; they focus on the green as their goal. At the same time they are mindful of the bunkers and where they are. Should an expert golfer land in a bunker, they have tried and tested strategies for getting out and back on track to the green.

Why am I telling you this? Well, a great many people I have spoken to about investing just can't get past their worries of being left with a house and nobody living in it. That just won't happen if you have bought in the right place, for the right tenant, and at the right price in relation to the rent you know you can get. When you have several properties in a portfolio the problem is not so great. You can take advantage of the property being empty and spruce it up and check it over. Have a plan ready to go into action.

Clean the house from top to bottom. I don't mean do it yourself – have a cleaning company you can trust and just call them straight away. Give the whole place a lick of paint – again, don't use your time, have someone you can rely on. Check everything is working: boiler, TV aerial, cooker and so on. Take new photos for marketing the property and get it back onto the market straight away.

SUMMARY

This chapter has been all about the tenants. I gave you all the basics you need to be able to deal with tenants. You discovered that more people than ever before are expecting to rent, and that means that it's very easy to find tenants and not have voids. In relation to our strategy – you learnt that there is a difference between investing for capital growth and investing for cash flow. I pointed out that investing for capital growth is just gambling because you don't know when or even if that growth will happen. When you invest for cash flow you get an immediate gain and when the capital growth occurs you can leverage that as well. I explained that voids are nothing to be afraid of because you have learnt how to buy the right property in the right location and let it at the right price for the market. I included a little bit of mindset stuff in order to get you focusing on filling your property with tenants. Then, you learnt about getting tenants out. It's not that hard when you know how to set things up in the first place. You read that things can be easier when you use agents but that it's up to you to check that they are good professional agents who are members of a trade association that guarantees their standards, and you should check that they have client accounts to protect the deposits. Lastly, I encouraged you to get a strategy together for void periods so that they don't last too long.

STEVE'S TOP TIPS

1. YIELD (this is the formula for a rough calculation of gross yield) is rent multiplied by 12, divided by purchase price, multiplied by 100.

2. You should be looking for a result of 8.5% or higher to be certain that you will make money every month.

3. Make sure you know all the costs of running your investments so that you know if you are making a profit.

4. Investing for capital growth is just gambling, but investing for income is future-proofing.

5. NEVER, EVER hand over your keys to potential tenants until you have:

   - A signed tenancy agreement
   - The deposit
   - The first month's rent

6. Warning! When advertising a vacancy you must: explain any charges or fees attached to applying for the tenancy and you must have an EPC (Energy Performance Certificate).

7. The law also requires you to hold a gas safety certificate and it must be renewed every year.

8. Best tenants are: blue collar workers, working families and young professionals.

9. Choose tenants carefully; be confident that there are plenty out there.

10. It's easy to vet tenants; just get their address details for the past three years and hand over to a vetting agency and wait for the results.

11. Don't accept cash for bypassing the application process and don't allow tenants to move furniture or any other possessions in before the start date of the tenancy agreement.

12. The best tenants to accept are the people who turn up on time, dress tidily and can prove regular work. It's okay to ask to see recent bank accounts.

13. Always serve a section 21 notice at the beginning of the tenancy – you don't have to use it but it will speed up the process of evicting them should you need to later.

14. Get a proven, well-established AST, and for further advice visit www.steve-evans.org.

15. When your property falls empty have a strategy for turning it around quickly.

EXTRACTING CAPITAL

WHY RECYCLE YOUR CAPITAL?

This chapter is the most exciting part of my whole PROP model – This is where we do the recycling. This is where it gets sexy!

My PROP System

Okay, we're nearly there with my PROP model.
Let's have a little recap.

P. Purchase

We bought our property from a motivated seller below its potential value.

R. Refurbish

We did it out in nice simple plain colours, put in a new boiler, kitchen and bathroom.

O. Occupy

We carefully selected a nice working family and they are paying their rent happily.

P. Pull the money out!

Now we're going to get our deposit back and maybe even make a bit of extra cash! (Yippee)

I hope by now I have got you loosened up when it comes to thinking about value? Value is completely subjective. It is all about supply and demand, and, in terms of property value, it's about who wants to live where and when. You should by now be getting to know the value of property in your area. However, I bet you don't know it as well today as you will this time next year. It is completely fluid and you must learn the micro movements in your chosen area. Remember "shiny objects?" They exist here too. Don't get concerned about the value of property anywhere else in the country; keep your focus on where you invest and know it well, and know it better than anyone else around you because that intimate knowledge will stand you in good stead when it comes to this part of the strategy.

I know that at the time of writing, banks have taken quite a pounding and a lot of people are looking for and finding alternatives, but that takes time and learning. It is also fraught with unforeseen problems and changes in rules. So, I'm sticking with traditional lending as my model for financing your property portfolio. I believe that banks are far too well ingrained into our financial system to be going away anytime soon, so let's get into the mindset of bankers.

Let us think now about what is happening here. There are two parties involved in the financing of property. The investor (you) and the banker. As in all negotiations we need to step back and look at what each party wants from the transaction.

First, you, the investor. You have £50,000 and you want to build a portfolio of properties that will create cash flow to provide you with some extra income in your retirement.

Next we have the banker. They need to lend out money to get a return on it, which they do in the form of an interest charge.

Our banker can lend to all sorts of people and enterprises, so they can choose the best one for their business. Broadly speaking they have the choice of either lending to other businesses, people who are employed (in the form of personal loans) or property (in the form of mortgages).

What does our banker know about the risks involved with each of their options? Well, lending to businesses is very risky and there are no guarantees that they will get the return they need. Personal loans are okay but they are short-term and there's no telling when, how or who will want to borrow how much and for how long. Compare that against lending on property.

Bankers know that when you come to them asking to borrow money to buy property, you are asking them to put money into one of the safest vehicles to invest in in the UK. They know that you will be borrowing for between 20 and 30 years. They know that really, it's the tenants who are footing the bill and even if you get it wrong someone can take it over and run with it.

So, how are our negotiations going? Well, the banker is looking upon your proposal of investing in property favourably and you are happy with their terms, so, as long as you can agree on the value, it's game-on. And what's so brilliant about this is that the banker is so positive about this venture that they are willing to lend you 75% of the value. In what other business proposal would they give you 75%? Imagine telling our banker that your business proposal is that you are going to put that money on the stock market – would they still offer you 75%?

Okay, so now you and the banker are agreed that property is the way to go, all you have to do is agree the price, the value of the property in question. That is the issue I am going to explore in this chapter.

Reuse of Capital

The reason investors like me and you need to get this strategy right is because we only have a finite amount of money to invest and it does run out from time to time. Therefore, we need a system that can reuse the original pot. We need to put the money in and then take it out again. It won't always go the way we want it to and we won't always agree on the value, but if we keep focused and plan carefully we will win.

Because bankers like property they are happy to invest at a very high level. That means that you only have to put in 25% of the purchase price. When that purchase price is 25% lower than the real, achievable value of that property then you can get the bank to agree on that higher value later, after you've made some improvements that justify the increase in value. This is where you need to know the value of comparable property in the same area. Only when you know what a property is worth can you know when you are looking at a bargain. Someone once said, "Start with the end in mind". That's exactly what you must do in investing – know what the ultimate value of the property should be and ensure that you can get it.

Reduce Risk to Capital

Business owners and investors the world over look for yield or ROI (Return on Investment). Put simply it means how much am I putting in and how much am I getting back? Another way of describing my PROP model is "no money left in", which means that what I attempt to do with financing an investment property is to have none of my own money left in that property, but still be getting a monthly income out after all costs. This is known as getting an infinite return on my investment because I have taken all the money out via revaluation.

When an investor achieves a state of having no money left in the deal, they have very little too lose. Obviously this requires the rent to be paid and all of the running costs to be met. Provided that you do that then you can't suffer repossession or bankruptcy.

Tax Benefits – Good Debt: Bad Debt

When I was a child growing up in the '60s, I was learning from my parents that you only had something when you had the money for it – debt was perceived to be bad and to be avoided at all costs. When my father wanted to buy his own home he got advice from his employer, the Metropolitan Police in London, and they told him that the mortgage should only cost about the same as one week's pay. My, how things have changed. If he could see me now he'd have an absolute fit! Almost all of the property I own except for my home has around 75% debt against it and I will go on borrowing that way for as long as I can.

The kind of debt an investor has secured against their property is often referred to as "good debt". So, what is bad debt then? Well, in order to answer that let's define good debt. It's really quite simple: good debt is debt that is secured against something that the lenders can sell and recover their money, should they need to. Bad debt is all those other unsecured loans that a lot of lenders spend a lot of time and money trying to get you to take out. Store cards, and unsecured personal loans to buy things like cars and furniture or holidays. Unsecured loans taken out to purchase liabilities (things that cost you money and never pay you money back). Then of course, there are credit cards. These are slightly different because it depends what you are buying with them – I can use a credit card to put down a 10% deposit on a property at auction and because that property is going to make me money it is good debt because there is an exit strategy. My exit strategy is that I will finance that purchase with a mortgage later and that will pay off the credit card.

As far as the tax man is concerned, good debt is debt on your portfolio that you can claim quite legitimately as costs against your income. You are entitled to claim the cost of borrowing, that is the interest on your mortgages, and as you should only be getting interest only mortgages you can claim all of the costs.

For inheritance tax planning there is a huge advantage to owing money on your portfolio and that is that you can keep the value of the cash in your estate below the inheritance tax threshold, and so save your beneficiaries an enormous tax bill that might otherwise cause them to have to sell the very property that is generating them the income you wanted them to have.

EXTRACTING CAPITAL

The Six Month Rule

At the time of writing, a slight obstacle to the PROP model is that the lenders do not current-ly allow investors to refinance within six months of becoming the owner of the property. This is a general rule set by the lenders and we have to work with it – there is no point in arguing with them. It just means that when you buy a property you will have to wait six months before you can refinance it.

Refinancing Strategy

In plain English, you're buying a house that is worth £100,000 for £75,000. You borrow 75% of your purchase price which gives you £52,250. You put in £22,750 and then spend £10,000 making your investment £32,750. Later you go back to the bank and borrow 75% of £100,000, giving you £75,000. Now take away your original mortgage (because you're taking out a new one) of £52,250, leaving you with £22,750, your deposit back out ready for the next!

At this point you need to think about your ongoing cash flow plans. You now need to think about what sort of mortgage suits your situation. Do you want a fixed rate for as long as you can get so that you know the costs for three, five, or ten years hence? Or would you prefer to be able to take advantage of capital growth whenever it happens?

There is a problem with signing up to a very long

term mortgage and that is that you won't be able to pull any more cash out until the end of the fixed rate. As I am writing this I have one property that has a two-year fixed mortgage and the value is rising day by day. It's frustrating because I can't take advantage of that growth until the end of the fixed rate. Instead, I am planning what I'll do when the fixed period is over.

Valuation

Remember I said at the beginning of this chapter that you need to know your area better than anybody else? Well, let's think about what that really means. You need to be on Rightmove every day: www.rightmove.com.

And you should be going to and talking to the agents every day so that you can see the difference between asking prices and selling prices. You need to figure out which roads people want to live in. Also, know and understand tenants – where do they like to live and work? The valuers will be looking at the rentable value as well as the market value, so know how much rent you can get.

When you have a potential deal, look around Rightmove and find out what comparable properties have sold for in the last two years. Also, you can go to Zoopla: www.zoopla.co.uk.

There you can get valuations by entering all sorts of details about your target property. You can even get an idea about what kind of difference the improvements you have in mind will make to the potential value. All you have to do is fill in a form on the site. If your house doesn't have double glazing, put it in on the form and see what a difference it would make.

Keep a record of all that you find out about your comparable – it will be useful later.

HOW TO REFINANCE

This is the part where you need an expert in your team. Don't try to do this yourself, because the market and the rules change all the time. Companies come and go and their products change every month.

Select the Right Product

When you go to your broker and ask for details of products they will give you a mind boggling load of figures and different options. You need to know what you want to do, and this is where the strategy helps you to find your way through the confusion.

The first thing the strategy tells you is that you want an interest only buy to let mortgage, and here's why.

Interest only mortgages are perfect for investing because you will never, ever in your lifetime, or your beneficiaries' lifetimes, want to sell the property! So you won't ever need to pay off the original loan, you will just keep on changing when you, "P", pull money out and when the time comes to hand it all over, you can assign it over to someone else.

Remember that you will want to refinance after six months, so you don't want a fixed period at this point – you only want that when everything is complete and you have tenants in. You may find that a light refurbishment product is available. These are good because they allow you to get started on the refurbishment at a lower initial rate and increase it once the property is ready to let.

Most of what your broker will offer you will be around fees and charges, and you will have to look at a spreadsheet over and over again because it will be full of swings and roundabouts. You will be faced with different interest rates, different valuation fees and different brokerage fees. There are flat administration fees and there are percentage fees. I'm sorry, but at this point you are on your own; it just depends on what's comfortable for you at the time. One thing I can say is that the more you use your chosen broker, the lower their fees will become. It's also good to use the same broker several times because they know your history and therefore they know which lenders will work best for you. Remember that your broker should be someone who has investment properties themselves, or is able to prove to you that they have clients with portfolios.

Work with the Valuer

Every time you apply to borrow money, the lenders will send out a valuer. When you first buy your property you don't need to do much in terms of getting on with them, because you have agreed a price with the vendor and it should be significantly lower than others like it in the same area. It's a different story, however, when you go for the remortgage later – you're going to need to make sure you get the valuation you want.

Now's the time to bring in all that comparable information you gathered before you did the deal. When you book the valuation visit make sure you can attend. You will need to strike a balance between getting on well and creating rapport, and telling the surveyor the value of the property. The way to do that is to make some small talk and see if you can find some sort of common ground, and then when the time is right offer them your file with the evidence in. The last bit is tricky and won't work on some occasions. It's worth dropping into the conversation things like "I saw one just like this around the corner in Acacia Avenue that sold for £111,000 last month". This is known as social proof. If you're going to have a go at it make sure it's true – the surveyor has access to more information than you and they will quickly know if you're trying to pull the wool over their eyes. All you are attempting to do is save them a bit of time. The last time I did this, the surveyor thanked me and said that I had saved him a load of time, and he also remarked that they were the same sources of information that he would have used. Naturally if you've saved the surveyor some time you will get your offer more quickly.

Extract Your Capital

Now that you have jumped through all of the hoops it's almost time to celebrate. Just hold on a little longer, because after the valuation is done you must wait for the offer to come through. Sometimes the lenders will come back to you via your broker and ask all sorts of odd questions. This is where your broker needs to know all there is to know about you. Be patient and just tell them everything they need to know. This is where you will find out if you have any skeletons in your financial cupboard, so before you get to this point find out how your credit rating is doing. If you've had any associations with anyone who has a bad score it could go against you, so I recommend joining one of the agencies that can help you clean up any issues from your past.

Okay, congratulations! You've just refinanced your first investment property and you now have the money back in the bank ready to do another!

SUMMARY

In this chapter, I showed you the biggest trick of the trade. How you pull your money back out. You learnt that bankers will lend 75% of the money for your investment, and that means that bankers regard property as an extremely safe investment. You read about keeping up with, and making yourself an expert on, the values both of property sales and rents in your area. We looked at what good debt and bad debt are and you discovered that it is okay to have 75% debt on your portfolio. You learnt that the important thing is to focus on return on investment, that is, how much of your own money is left in and how much cash you are getting each month. Of course, I talked a lot about mortgages – you learnt that the best for this strategy are buy to let interest only mortgages. You also discovered the reason for gathering all that price comparison data – it's all about getting the valuation you want at the end of the process.

STEVE'S TOP TIPS

1. Know your values and get plenty of comparisons.

2. Borrow 75% loan to value – that's the sweet spot between the lender's comfort zone and you making cash flow.

3. Keep to the strategy for revaluing and you can reuse your capital.

4. Every time you revalue and pull cash out you are both reducing the money you have at risk and increasing the return you're getting on that money. When you have no money left in the property your returns are infinite.

5. Good debt, bad debt. Bad debt is things like store cards, personal loans and purchases on credit cards that don't earn you anything. Good debt is where your money is secured against a true asset that is something that is providing you with an income.

6. Having good debt against your portfolio reduces your tax liabilities both for inheritance tax and income tax.

7. The six month rule. Lenders won't let you borrow a second time until you have owned the property for six months.

8. Get a good understanding of all the different kinds of mortgage products so that you know what suits you best for the long-term.

9. Know the rental values for your area because the lender's valuer will find out what they are and base your loan on them.

10. Keep records of values to show the valuer later.

11. Only use interest only mortgages. You will never need to sell so you will never need to pay off the original loan.

12. Make the first mortgage, the one to buy the property, a standard variable because you will want to change product after six months.

13. Keep using the same mortgage broker and their fees should come down. It's also helpful to be using someone who knows you well and can represent you with the lenders.

14. At the revaluation, seek to get a good rapport with the surveyor, drop in social proof and gently offer your dossier on recent values.

15. Now just pop your money back in the bank and do it all again.

MANAGING YOUR PORTFOLIO

WHY IS MANAGEMENT IMPORTANT?

There are two distinct areas in managing a property portfolio, and you need to be aware of both. On one hand you have the obvious and quite demanding issues of your tenants, and on the other and quite often neglected hand there is the property itself. Both are very important and you should plan and set up systems for dealing with them. In this chapter I'll give you some pointers and things to be aware of in order to make running things on a daily basis smooth and profitable.

Once you have a couple of properties under your hat you'll need to think about how much you should be doing yourself or how much to leverage. What does leverage even mean? Well, in engineering terms, it means that you use a small movement in one part of the operation to cause a much larger movement somewhere else. In management terms, it's getting someone else to do something so that you can concentrate on another part of the operation. The people I learnt my systems from taught me that you should start your day in the following order:

- Leverage – get others to do the things you're not needed for.

- Manage – supervise the things that you need to have some input in but can get others to do.

- Do – do the things that no one else can do.

When you have just a couple of properties it may not seem exactly overwhelming to check in the odd tenant from time to time, do the odd visual inspection or get a paintbrush out here and there. As your portfolio grows you may find that these little jobs suddenly take over your life and you have no time to enjoy any benefits from this vehicle of wealth creation. I have met many a landlord who has got to the point of feeling overwhelmed and wanting to sell their entire portfolio.

Remember this is meant to be a pension pot – that is, something that will provide you with an income no matter what else you are doing. Want to go on a world cruise when you retire from business? Well, get things set up well and you can go off and take three years out without losing any income!

Now I'm not suggesting that you don't have anything to do with managing your portfolio – far from it. I'm simply saying that you need to start planning to get to the point where your portfolio is running on autopilot and you can just tweak it occasionally and steer it from time to time so that it is a pleasure to have it there in the background.

The more you know and understand how the day-to-day running of a property portfolio should work, the more you can leverage it. The more you know what to do and how it should be done whenever a problem arises, the more accurately you can direct someone else to do it and know whether they are doing it properly. The better your portfolio is run, the more money you will make from it in the long-term.

Maintain Control

Make sure you are well-educated in all of the areas of property and tenant management so that you can be certain that the people you employ to look after your investments are doing things correctly and helping you to achieve your goals.

Let your agents/managers know what your long-term plans are so that they know what areas of maintenance to look out for. When you have voids, check the advertising and viewing details with those agents to show them that you are watching them and that if they don't perform they'll lose the job.

Optimising Cashflow

Your job should ideally be keeping records of what is happening. For example how much rent is coming in and how much is going out in expenses so that you know in advance if any property is not making you money. You do not want to wait until you do your tax return at the end of the year to find out that you have overspent and made a loss.

If you have an HMO, keep track of the meter readings because those tenants don't pay any attention to their usage of electricity, gas or water!

Preventing Problems

Keeping yourself aware of how everything is going helps to avoid unwelcome surprises. Making regular visual inspections, either by yourself or via an agent, will help to make you aware of any structural or tenancy issues.

PROPERTY MANAGEMENT

Condition of Fabric

Once you have done a couple of refurbishments you should have tradespeople you can trust. In my business I have a project manager who I know gives me honest opinions about the condition of each property. I have a plan for general issues like replacing boilers or repairing roofs, so that when I do the refinance part of the strategy I use a little of the cash to make repairs.

Draw up a long-term plan of replacing the things you didn't need to at the time of refurbishment but are aware need doing sometime.

Buildings Insurance

You are legally responsible for the structures you

own. You must get yourself insured to cover the barest minimum of your responsibilities. You may be expected or even required by your lenders to insure the building. You are not responsible for the tenants' belongings and you should make them aware of that. Let them know that they must take out their own contents insurance.

Because I supply the floor coverings, and sometimes, the curtains and white goods, I often use a policy that includes things that are fixed to the property. I would also strongly advise you to have accidental damage cover too – this will prevent you having to argue with tenants and insurers about what caused the claim. If you want to get your premiums down and you have a good maintenance team, increase the excess.

There are several companies that offer landlords portfolio insurance and they are quite easy to find, but if you want recommendations just visit my website: www.steve-evans.org.

Letting Agents

I've said it before and I'll say it again – get yourself educated in terms of managing tenants so that you know whether you've got a good agent or not, because they vary tremendously in their levels of service. By knowing how things should be done you'll know if they are being done. I once had a phone call from an agent who was part of a national organisation, to tell me that the gas safety certificate would expire within 24 hours, and that was the first I'd heard about it. Luckily I had a gas engineer removing two gas fires in an empty house that day, so I was able to phone him and ask him to go and do the certificate there and then. Otherwise, I would have been in breach of the law for not having an up-to-date certificate. That is exactly the kind of administrative error I employ an agent to avoid for me, so I fired them.

Services

Whether you have single let properties or large HMOs you will have to deal with utilities. The single most common mistake landlords make here is with pre-pay meters. There are two things you should know about pre-pay meters: 1. The unit price is always significantly higher, 2. They are the most common mechanism used by the utility companies to recover debt. The way they do this is by adding the debt to the client's account so that every time they top up the pre-pay card and put it back into the meter, the meter takes some of that debt off the card. In other words, you may buy a property that has pre-pay meters installed and you pop off down to the local convenience store with the card in your hot little hand to pop £20.00 on it so that you can get going with the wallpaper stripping and making comforting cups of tea for the friends and family you roped in to help. Suddenly, all the lights go out and you find there's nothing left on the meter except emergency cover. That is because the previous owners or tenants left owing money on them and the meter is taking that debt off every time you top up the card.

The way to get round this is to contact the utility companies the day you get the keys. Call them and tell them that you are the new owners and the utility provider will send you out a new key that will zero the debt. They will ask you if you have an address for the previous people. If you have got the solicitor's details from the sale it would be a good idea to pass that on to them and you shouldn't hear any more about it.

I like to set all my properties up with the same provider so that I know who to call to sort out any problems. However, when you install your tenants, in the case of a single let, they are entitled to change to whichever provider they choose. It's different when you are dealing with a multi-let property. Tenants in a shared house prefer to have just one bill – your rent. So it is common practice for HMO landlords to pay all the utilities and put a fair usage clause in the agreement. If you do this, you must keep track of the meter readings and warn the tenants if they are getting close to the limit.

For more information and to learn how you could make a little extra cash from your utilities, visit my website at www.steve-evans.org.

If you plan to be an HMO landlord, you need to organise paying the community tax as well as the water and TV licence. You will also find that your tenants expect Sky and very good broadband. If you try to keep these costs down by making the tenants pay for them, you will struggle to fill your house and it will cost you in the long-run.

TENANT MANAGEMENT

Letting Agents

Great agents are worth their weight in gold. This is the part of leverage where you should be able to leverage someone else to do the job, leave them to get on with it and just send you the money every month. However, it doesn't always work like that, so I suggest that you get to know them all by trying one or two out. When you find one that works for you, give them everything to manage.

When it comes to letting out your property, get them all round to give you an idea of the rent achievable. Don't just go for the one who offers you the most; you can offer it to all of them and see which one performs the best – i.e., decide what price you want to offer the property at and ask all your agents to advertise it. Whichever agent gets you a tenant first should be offered the job of managing it.

Make sure that you are easy for them to communicate with. There's nothing worse for an agent than a client who is hard to contact. Your agent is your frontline protection from day-to-day running issues and they need to know what you would do in every circumstance. The more you talk with them, the less you will have to talk with tenants, and believe me, it's a lot easier to talk to an agent.

Always keep your agents informed about your business overall because they might know people who are tired of being landlords and want to sell. They will also be after more business and that might help you to keep costs down or at least get a better service.

Voids

We have covered this subject earlier in this book but it is relevant here too. Voids are just a part of the business and nothing to be afraid of. The way to deal with them is to have systems in place and swing them into action as soon as you can.

As soon as your existing tenants give you notice, start advertising. Find a great cleaning company and get them in there immediately. Get your maintenance team in straight away too and also take the chance to get some up-to-date photos.

Having a void is also a good time to put your rent up. It is much easier to come down if no one takes it rather than trying to push it up if it goes quickly because you priced it too low.

Landlord-Tenant Relationships

The law requires you to make available a genuine address with contact details for your tenants. This is in addition to your agent's contact details. It doesn't have to be your home but it mustn't be a PO Box either. Most of us start off by dealing directly with the tenants and this is a good way to understand them. Tenants are not like property investors or business owners, and they have a very different mindset. For example, I once attempted to persuade a young couple not to install pre-pay meters for their utilities as the unit cost was a lot more than if they set up a budget account with the supplier. They didn't care at all about the unit price; they were only concerned about putting a set amount in the meter every week. Getting the right kind of rapport with your tenants is a skill and it's one worth investing in. If you don't know much about NLP (Neuro-Linguistic Programming), I suggest that you read a bit about the basics and maybe do an introductory course just to learn rapport techniques.

Really the state of rapport you want to achieve with tenants is one of mutual respect with a little authority thrown in. You want them to like you a little, but feel that if they overstep the mark they could lose out. I had a tenant in one of my multi-let properties once who offered to do some maintenance jobs and also suggested I pay him to clean the house. I resisted, and when he fell behind on his rent I was very glad I didn't feel I owed him anything. In fact, because I had to send him a detailed statement on his debt which I reserve the right to charge for, he refused for quite some time to pay the £10.00 fee. Eventually, after pointing out the section in the contract regarding extra fees he paid up and apologised.

STRATEGY MANAGEMENT

Reviewing Goals

Goal setting is like playing crown green bowling: you have your target, the jack, and you aim your ball at it. However, the ball does not go in a straight line and there are other balls in the way. Sometimes other players' balls move the jack or get in the way of your shot. Therefore, you must change your approach and adjust your strategy as these things affect your plans.

In building your property portfolio, things will change that are beyond your control. People will do things that affect what you were trying to achieve and governments will make differences that will also affect your outcome. The people who succeed in this business are those who learn from their and other people's mistakes. The successful people are the ones who keep going and overcome their problems. Achievers are not dissuaded by other people. Achievers look for reasons why, not reasons why not!

To keep focused on your goals you should have a clear picture of them. You must focus on them and really tune into what you want. You need to have really strong feelings about where you want to go and grasp them with both hands. Involve your loved ones. Everybody you care about, who will listen, should know what it is you're working towards so that they understand your reasons for doing the things you are doing.

From time to time you should take a step back and review where you are. Ask yourself what it was you set out to do and look at the current position to see if it is aligned with the plan. If you find that you've not achieved everything you set out to do, work out what got in the way and figure out whether that problem can be dealt with, or if it has to be lived with and the goals realigned. If you find that the goals were surpassed easily, and you didn't even notice that you'd achieved what you set out to achieve, set yourself a new set of goals and enjoy pushing ahead! The greatest achievers in history never sat back and contemplated their navels; they always had more they wanted to do and that's what drove them to great things.

Refinancing Where Needed

One of the most important parts of my PROP strategy, the part that gets you infinite returns, is the "P" pull money out part. To take full advantage of this part you must keep yourself aware of property values where your portfolio is. Get estate agents in to give you their opinion and check out all the resources available to know what prices houses are fetching. At the same time, keep on top of rent values so that you are getting enough rent to cover the cost of revaluing your house and pulling money out. Remember, you don't want to leave behind a large amount of cash that will just go to the government and not directly benefit your loved ones.

It is by doing this part of the PROP strategy that my own clients pay me if they ask for payment terms. Because I know the system works if a client hasn't got enough cash to pay my fees as they go, we draw up an agreement that is tied to the property and when the revaluation takes place I get paid.

Growing Portfolio

Perhaps I should call this part the snowball effect. To achieve the ultimate goal of financial freedom you should have a completely automated system that keeps on producing more money every day. By now, you have your team in place and systems for running them so it is easy to revalue a house and put the money down as a deposit on another. Also at this point, you will probably be paying tax on your income from the portfolio, so it would be quite handy to have the occasional big expense to reduce that tax liability. Remember that the whole idea is to buy and hold. Never sell any of your properties because they should be creating income for you. Just add until you are getting a great return and hold forever.

SUMMARY

In this last chapter, we discussed managing and maintaining things in order to build on them. Once more, I've got you to consider using leverage – getting others to do things for you so that you are free to live the life you dream of. However, you've learnt that you must first get yourself educated – you need to know how your property and your tenants should be managed in order to know that the people you are leveraging are doing a good job. You've read about my ideas on property maintenance – how it's good to have a plan for long-term repairs and that you communicate that plan with your team so that they understand where you are heading. When it comes to protecting yourself and others you learnt that it is good to insure your property as a landlord and how you can provide the right cover and keep the cost down at the same time. Then there was something no one told me – pre-pay meters collect debt. I explained how you avoid getting charged for the previous people's utility debts. And for the multi-let houses you learnt all about what utilities you should provide and how you can keep them under control. You read, too, about the relationship between landlords and their tenants, and I recommended that you consider learning some basic relationship and communications skills. This will enable you to build the ideal relationship with your tenants. For the times when there are no tenants, you read more about having a strategy ready to swing into action to lessen the impact of no rent coming in. You learnt that you should have in place: a cleaning company, your maintenance team, and be ready to take pictures. The close of this chapter and this book is the subject closest to my heart – goal setting. You discovered that setting goals is like playing bowls. I explained that even though things can change, by keeping focused on your goals, you can change and adapt to stay on target. Lastly you read that to grow your portfolio you should by now have an automated system that makes it easy to keep adding properties to your portfolio and grow your income.

STEVE'S TOP TIPS

1. Be aware that the fabric of the property needs managing as well as the tenants. Have plans in place to deal with issues arising from maintenance and repairs.

2. When setting up regular systems for management think leverage.

    - Leverage – get others to do the things you're not needed for.

    - Manage – supervise the things that you need to have some input in but can get others to do.

    - Do – do the things that no one else can do.

3. Get educated in the field of tenant management so that you know if your agent is doing their job correctly.

4. Communicate with your letting agent and ensure that they know your business well

so that if they can help/advise on the areas you have plans for, they will.

5. Keep good records of all costs so that you know if a property is not performing and can see where any problems might lie.

6. Make sure you or your agent carry out regular visual inspections.

7. Review the condition of all your properties with your builder so that you can have a long-term maintenance programme.

8. You must get landlords' liability insurance to cover your responsibilities for the building and it is advisable to get a policy that covers the internal fixings like flooring and curtain rails.

9. As soon as you buy a property, contact the utility provider. If the property has pre-pay meters make sure they send you new payment cards to avoid being charged for previous owners debts.

10. Get several agents in and ask them all to advertise your property and give the

management to the one who gets you the tenants at the right price.

11. Communicate well with your agent and you will not have to communicate with your tenants.

12. Have a system in place to cope with voids. Get cleaners in, put a maintenance team in and take new photos.

13. Whenever a tenant leaves, put the price up for the next. You can always come down, but it's much harder to put the price up when you have tenants in place.

14. Learn NLP basics so that you understand simple rapport techniques.

15. Be approachable for tenants but maintain an air of authority.

16. Review your goals from time to time. Check where you have got to and plan where you are going at least once a year.

17. Be an achiever who learns from your mistakes as well as other people's.

18. Always study property values in your area and know what rents people are achieving so that you can get your property revalued whenever there is an increase.

BOOK SUMMARY

Chapter one is all about the building blocks

I talked about property being a much better investment than a pension fund. I also looked at assessing your assets and what exactly assets and liabilities are. You learnt that liabilities are any possessions you have that cost you money, and assets are possessions you have that earn you money. I also explained that you are an ideal investor if you are a small-business owner with £50,000 cash available and an income of £30,000 or more. And you learnt that you can use equity in your home or raise the money from your business.

Chapter two is about the value of strategies

I explained how important they are, and how they keep you focused on your goals. We also covered setting goals and how to get connected to them using all your senses. We looked at the yield calculation that makes sure you buy at the right price to make a profit, and discussed the different types of tenant – discovering which work best for the PROP strategy.

Chapter three is about the value

I explained that the value of anything is how much someone who wants to buy is prepared to pay at the time someone else needs to sell. I explained that you are going to need to do a lot of hunting before you find your first bargain. It wasn't all bad news though, because I taught you how to spot the people who need to sell at a discount. I explained that there are people who have other criteria besides getting the highest price – people who sell for many other reasons not related to price at all. You read all about the different ways you can find the sellers who don't go to agents, get in ahead of the agents and offer a quick sale. You also learnt about all the different ways of up lifting the value of your property and you got my favourite calculation, the yield calculator – the way to work out very quickly in your head how much you should buy the house for . Lastly, I gave you a basic spreadsheet list of headings, which you should make sure you use because it will build into a comprehensive record of property values in your area.

Chapter four starts to look at the long-term plan in my strategy

You read about borrowing 75% of the value of your portfolio being the standard level for the investing industry, and how this means that you will reduce your income tax and your beneficiaries' inheritance tax when you're gone. I explained how inflation can wipe out debt. You learnt that you can create value by buying at a discount, extending or converting to create extra bedrooms or replacing things like kitchen/bathrooms or putting in a new central heating system. I also explained that decorating for tenants should be done simply and with plain magnolia-like colours and you learnt that it's okay to let tenants paint the odd wall themselves. When it comes to purchasing your property, I told you that you must have your paperwork ready and everything in place such as your ID for solicitors and mortgage brokers alike. With regard to negotiations, I pointed out that you must keep as quiet as possible and find out as much as possible before declaring your hand. You learnt that you should use your ears and mouth in proportion to each other – in other words, use your ears twice as much as your mouth. You learnt that open questions are the most effective to use when finding out something – open questions are questions that begin with W or H, such as who, what, where and when. On the subject of finance, I illustrated the power of leverage to explain how with a 25% deposit on £100,000 investment, you will make a 50% return when the property's value goes up by 10%.

Chapter five is all about the tenants

In this chapter I gave you all the basics you need to be able to deal with tenants. You discovered that more people than ever before are expecting to rent, and that means that it's very easy to find tenants and not have voids. In relation to our strategy, you learnt that there is a difference between investing for capital growth and investing for cash flow. I pointed out that investing for capital growth is just gambling because you don't know when, or even if, that growth will happen. When you invest for cash flow you get an immediate gain, and when the capital growth occurs you can leverage that as well. I explained that voids are nothing to be afraid of because you have learnt how to buy the right property in the right location, and let it at the right price for the market. I included a little bit of mind set stuff in order to get you focusing on filling your property with tenants. Then you learnt about getting tenants out. It's not that hard when you know how to set things up in the first place. You read that things can be easier when you use agents, but that it's up to you to check that they are good, professional agents who are members of a trade association that guarantees their standards, and you should check that they have client accounts to protect the deposits. Lastly, I encouraged you to get a strategy together for void periods so that they don't last too long.

Chapter six explained the biggest trick of the trade

You discovered how to pull your money back out. You learnt that bankers will lend 75% of the money for your investment, and that means that bankers regard property as an extremely safe investment. You read about keeping up with, and making yourself an expert on the values both of property sales and rents in your area. I looked at what good debt and bad debt are, and you discovered that it is okay to have 75% debt on your portfolio. You learnt that the important thing is to focus on return on investment – that is, how much of your own money is left in and how much cash are you getting each month. Of course, I talked a lot about mortgages – you learnt that the best for this strategy are buy to let interest only mortgages. You also discovered the reason for gathering all that price comparison data – it's all about getting the valuation you want at the end of the process.

Chapter seven, the last chapter, is all about managing and maintaining things

Once more I've been getting you to consider using leverage, getting others to do things for you so that you are free to live the life you dream of. However, you've also learnt that you must first get yourself educated – you need to know how your property and your tenants should be managed in order to know that the people you are leveraging are doing a good job. You also read about my ideas on property maintenance – how it's good to have a plan for long-term repairs and that you communicate that plan with your team so that they understand where you are heading. When it comes to protecting yourself and others you learnt that it is good to insure your property as a landlord and how you can provide the right cover and keep the cost down at the same time. Then there was something no one told me – pre-pay meters collect debt. I explained how you avoid getting charged for the previous people's utility debts. And for the multi-let houses, you learnt all about what utilities you should provide and how you can keep them under control. You read, too, about the relationship between landlords and their tenants, and I recommended that you consider learning some basic relationship and communications skills. This will enable you to build the ideal relationship with your tenants. For the times when there are no tenants, you read more about having a strategy ready to swing into action to lessen the impact of no rent coming in. You learnt that you should have in place: a cleaning company, your maintenance team, and be ready to take pictures. The close of this chapter and this book is the subject closest to my heart – goal setting. You discovered that setting goals is like playing bowls. I explained that even though things can change, by keeping focused on your goals, you can change and adapt to stay on target. Lastly, you read that to grow your portfolio you should by now have an automated system that makes it easy to keep adding properties to your portfolio and grow your income.

NEXT STEPS

Congratulations—by reading this book from start to finish you have taken action to get yourself ahead of the crowd. I have met many people who've got lots of wealth creation and personal development books on their shelves and they've not read a single one all the way through – you have and you should be pleased with that. You've probably kept reading because you found the content right for you – I expect you could relate to some or all of the comments I've made regarding pensions, planning for the future and taking action.

If you have taken action and started, congratulations; I hope you've achieved the same results or better than I have?

If you haven't managed to get started yet, then don't worry. I understand perfectly; a book is great to give you knowledge and information, but it doesn't get things done for you. Many people get started and hit an obstacle; I do know that the book isn't quite enough for some people. If you're someone who wants desperately to get started, but find that you're too busy, or you don't quite have the confidence to get started or something is blocking your progress and you can't find your way round it, get yourself along to my website (www. steve-evans.org), where you will find lots of help and resources to move you forward.

ABOUT THE AUTHOR

"I'm an advocate of self-employment and have considerable success in utilising property investment to overcome its shortcomings. Because I spend a lot of my time tuning into people and making things happen, I can easily help small-business owners to generate long-term cash flow, which will eliminate any pension shortfall. What really annoys me is that so many small-business owners have already been robbed of the opportunity to retire because of the lies they have been told about their pensions. I believe that everyone's future can be taken into their own hands. Opening my eyes to property investment has been my own salvation and I sincerely believe that the same strategy could benefit others too".

Steve Evans, 2014

Steve Evans was born in 1962. During his first year it was discovered that he had a rare eye condition which would eventually render him totally blind. Although he had some useful vision at primary school he very quickly fell behind the other kids, and by the time he was eight years old his determined mum got him registered blind, meaning he would have to go to a school that taught using Braille, white canes and a lot of audio.

As he headed towards the end of his time at school, he started to think about his options; he was great at sport, good at music and rubbish behind a desk! "I wanted to be a sound engineer but no one took that seriously. They just said, 'How would you tell the difference between a blue wire and a black wire?' Eventually he was introduced to piano tuning and he flourished. "I loved the idea of being self-employed and building my own business".

In 1978 Steve joined The Royal National College of the Blind in Hereford to study piano tuning, and in 1981 he qualified with honours and set out in the big wide world. "I was invincible; I was going to set the world alight!"

Since studying personal development and business building, Steve has learnt that being self-employed is different to building a business. "Looking back it is so obvious to me that just working as hard as you can, for as many hours as you can, will never be a business". He has learnt that leverage and creating systems is what builds a successful business. "I now know that a business is something you create that earns you money even when you are not there, even when you are on holiday, even when you're asleep!"

When he started out, Steve built his customer base up quite quickly. "To start with things went very well. I advertised in the local paper, I tendered contracts and, when I got really successful, I took out ads in the Yellow Pages".

Whilst still in his early 20s, he bought his first property and even took out his first pension plan. "How forward-thinking is that?" He can clearly recall what he was told when he took out the plan. "I remember the salesman saying, 'You'll actually be able to take out half the money when you're 50.' Well, that's been cancelled by the present government. I think it was when I was about 49 they raised the minimum age to 55".

Since then he has watched property more than double in value on average every ten years. The first flat he bought for £34,000 is now worth £360,000 30 years on.

During the same period, he has seen pensions rise for a short time, and then plummet. After starting and stopping his contributions for various reasons over the years, he got an IFA to pull together three separate policies. "He found that I had £36,000. We put that into one policy and it grew to £41,000, then down it went. It bottomed out at about £21,000". No way was he going to continue to pump money into that kind of loss!

Instead, he pursued his dream, his passion, and that was to find something that he could do to generate regular, recurring income that didn't require him to go out every day and do something physical that people would pay him once for and then he'd have to do it all over again to get any more money. No, there had to be something else, something self-perpetuating, something he could do just once, which would pay him over and over again.

He realised that people pay rent every month and they live in the same house for years at a time, so all he had to do was to get them paying their rent to him. "All I had to do was to learn how to buy the right properties, at the right price, in the right location!" He says, "Sounds simple? Well, it is, once you have learnt the system – get that right and the rest will follow".

Steve has spent several years and over £20,000 learning from the top experts in the UK and this has provided him with a portfolio of property worth over £1.2 million. It generates £67,300 income and he doesn't have to tune any more pianos!